TENACIOUS D

Transcribed by Jeff Jacobson

Cherry Lane Music Company
Director of Publications/Project Editor: Mark Phillips

ISBN 1-57560-812-X

Visit our website at www.cherrylane.com

THE GREATEST BAND ON EARTH

(as told by Tenacious D)

TenaciousD: Jack Black n Kyle Gass make up the Greatest Band in History Tenacious D. They started playing together in Kyle's studio apt on Cochran Ave in Los Angeles. No one could have ever dreamed of where their genius would take them but take them it did... Tenacious D played their first gig at Al's bar in downtown LA in 94; they were armed with only one song at the time. "Tribute" a tribute to the greatest song in the world that when once played...

TenaciousD: the small crowds brains collectively exploded!

TenaciousD: who are these two guys?

TenaciousD: why are they so....

TenaciousD: so...

Superflei2: so...

TenaciousD: well you fill in the adjective...

TenaciousD: but at that very first show there was a PECULIAR looking fellow one David Cross

TenaciousD: who said he enjoyed our little fandango and invited us to play a comedy show with him n some friends in Hwood

Superflei2: and that would be

TenaciousD: the Diamond Club

TenaciousD: doing a series of shows with Host Laura Milligan and such guest stars as Ben Stiller and Jeaneane Garafalo to name but a few

Superflei2: just a few

Superflei2: of course

TenaciousD: our little posse began what was to tcrmcd for bcttcr or worse the "alternative" comedy movement

TenaciousD: but The D was more...

TenaciousD: much more

TenaciousD: The D began to headline Comedy Night first at Pedros

Superflei2: then

TenaciousD: and then when it moved to Largo

TenaciousD: but whenever the D performed, people knew they were witnessing something special

TenaciousD: it was hard to describe...

Superflei2: but please do...

TenaciousD: "What is it....these two guys...

TenaciousD: playin acoustic guitars

TenaciousD: yet rockin harder

TenaciousD: than bands with thrice the volume?

TenaciousD: hold on

Superflei2: thrice volume...

TenaciousD: so hard

TenaciousD: Why was a live D show so compelling, the people asked, so entertaining so mind blowing so...so..so Rocking?

TenaciousD: It was alm

Superflei2: alm?

TenaciousD: sorry   It was almost impossible for people to explain the next day to their friends or co workers

Superflei2: i can't imagine the conversation by the water cooler!

TenaciousD: was it this wild lead singer with pipes of platinum?

Superflei2: or

TenaciousD: or was it the heavy set bald fellow churning out riffs of pure profundity?

TenaciousD: or was it some synergy created by these too unlikely rock gods that really couldn't be explained but had to

TenaciousD: be experienced LIVE and in person. Yes that is what it was!

TenaciousD: who knew that because Jack n Kyle were such uncompromising artists it would be years before they would submit to releasing their songs

TenaciousD: yeah yeah are you taking all this down?

Superflei2: i am!

Superflei2: keep rolling

TenaciousD: soon

TenaciousD: Bob Odenkirk n David Cross would want to exploit the D for their own devices

Superflei2: an evil plot?

TenaciousD: and take the D's natural magic, try n bottle it and put it on the small screen on pay cable

TenaciousD: what was created ignited the nation

Superflei2: into flames?

TenaciousD: anyone who was witness to the original HBO TV show was treated to nothing less than an entertainment revolution

TenaciousD: Jack Black and Kyle Gass have arrived

TenaciousD: to change the way we listen to sound

TenaciousD: to change the way we thought

Superflei2: think?

TenaciousD: to change the way we might eat a delicious meal

Superflei2: indeed

TenaciousD: but integrity came first as it always does with the D

TenaciousD: and all parties had to part ways

TenaciousD: the show that replaced the D? oh I don't know if you've heard of a little show called

TenaciousD: THE SOPRANOS!

Superflei2: hmmm...the 3 tenors?

TenaciousD: well Jack n Kyle had something to prove now

Superflei2: and

TenaciousD: so they staged a bidding war

TenaciousD: signed with Epic Records

TenaciousD: made a record with some wickedly talented dudes

TenaciousD: Dave Grohl, Page from Phish, Warren from the Vandals, Steve from Redd Kross and the Dust Bros. in the production seat

Superflei2: due Sept. 25th.......

TenaciousD: then Spumco, the creators of Ren & Stimpy, made a rockin' animated music video for their favorite love song

Superflei2: a silly love song?

TenaciousD: not silly, a deep love song called "Fuck Her Gently"

TenaciousD: wrote a movie

TenaciousD: due out next year

TenaciousD: and blah blah blag

TenaciousD: there done!

CONTENTS

KIELBASA

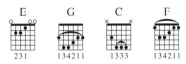

Words and Music by
Jack Black and Kyle Gass

Intro
Free time

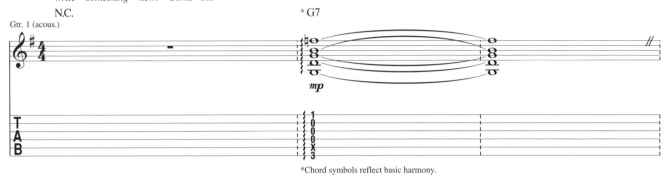

*Chord symbols reflect basic harmony.

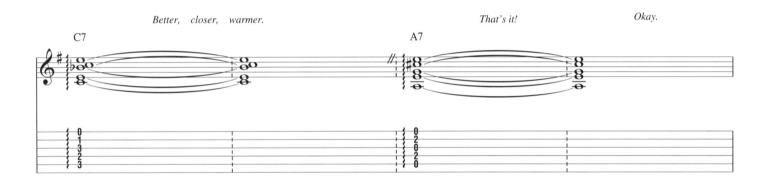

Moderately slow ♩ = 100

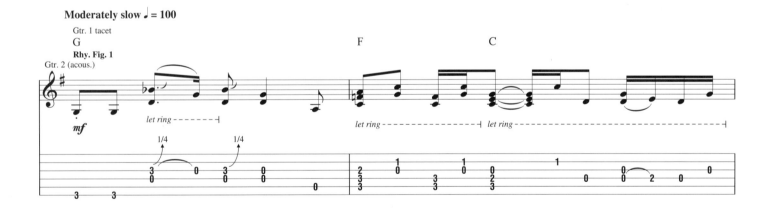

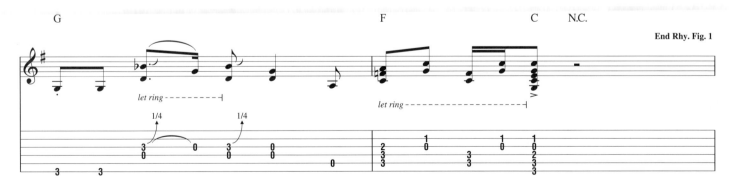

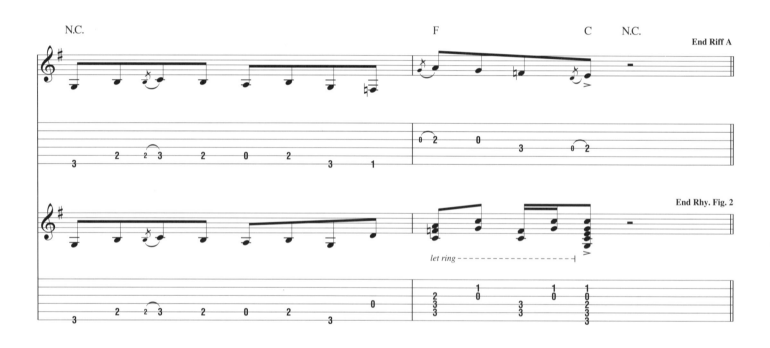

Verse

1. I love ___ ya, ba - by, but all I can think ___ a - bout is

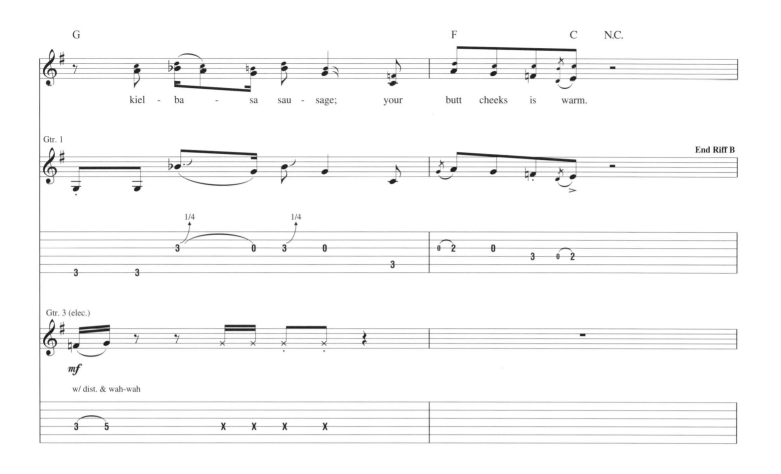

kiel - ba - sa sau - sage; your butt cheeks is warm.

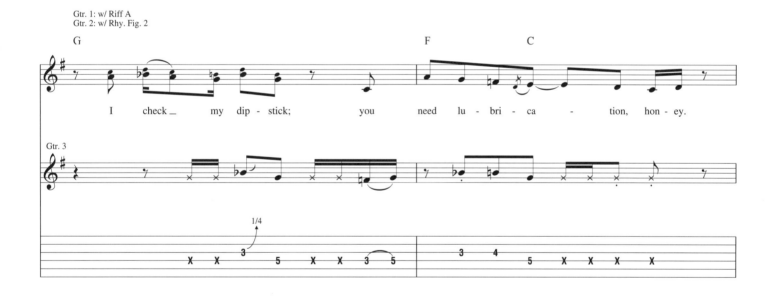

I check _ my dip - stick; you need lu - bri - ca - tion, hon - ey.

My kiel - ba - sa sau - sage has just got to per - form. Now get it on. ___

Guitar Solo

Gtr. 1: w/ Riff B

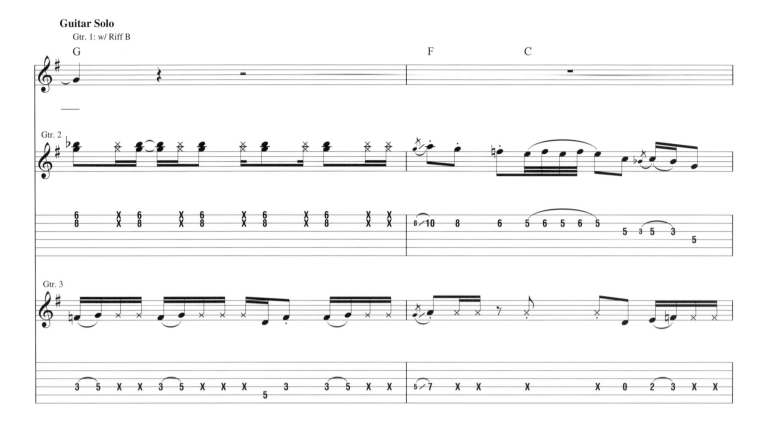

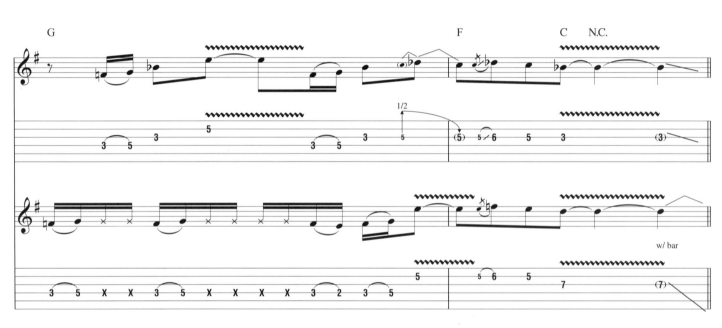

Verse

Gtr. 1: w/ Riff B
Gtr. 2: w/ Rhy. Fig. 1

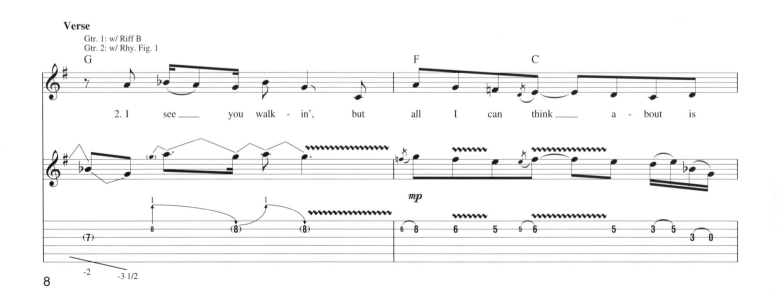

2. I see ____ you walk - in', but all I can think ____ a - bout is

8

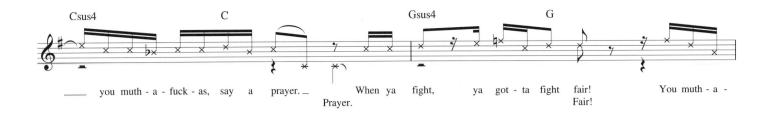

you muth-a-fuck-as, say a prayer. When ya fight, ya got-ta fight fair! You muth-a-

Prayer.   Fair!

fuck-a,   oh,   you muth-a-fuck-a.   You know what time it is?

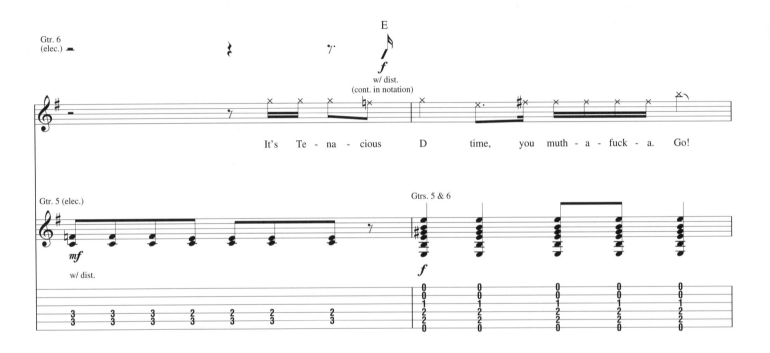

It's Te-na-cious   D   time,   you muth-a-fuck-a.   Go!

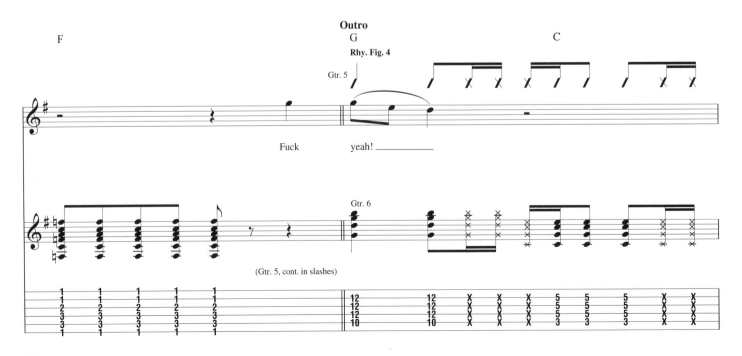

Fuck   yeah!

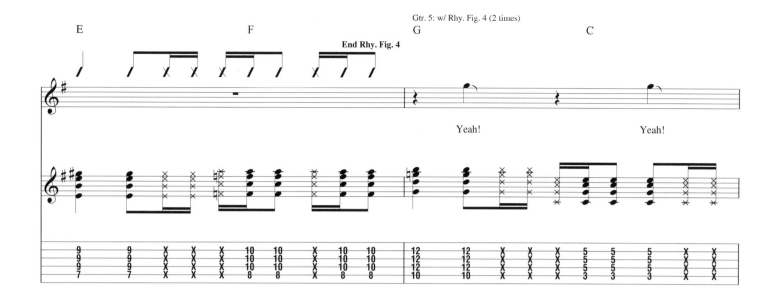

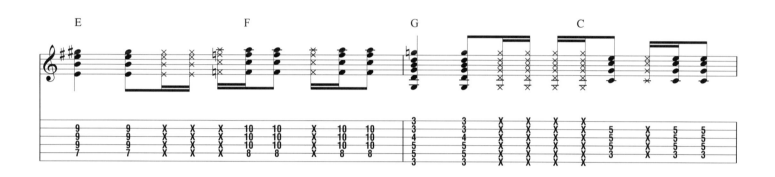

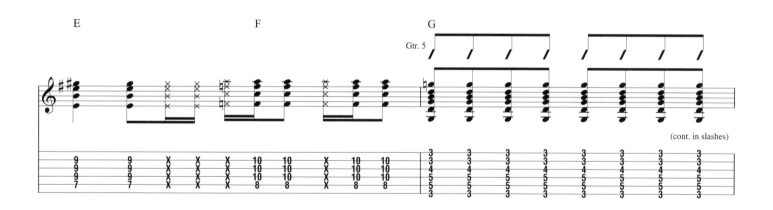

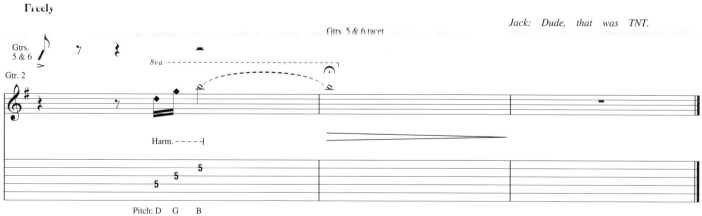

TRIBUTE

Words and Music by
Jack Black and Kyle Gass

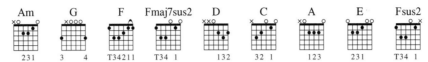

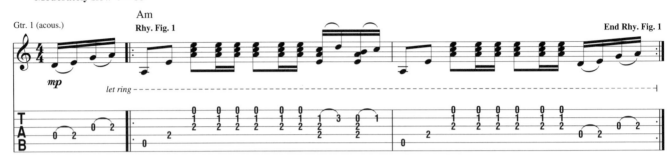

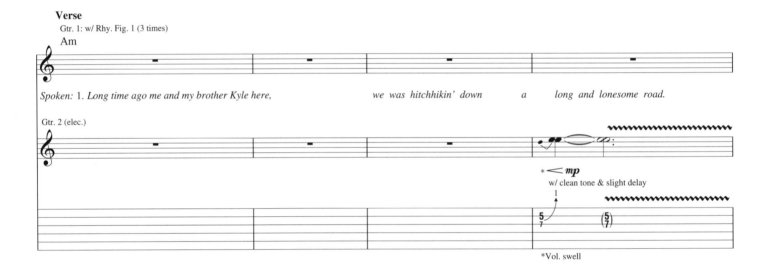

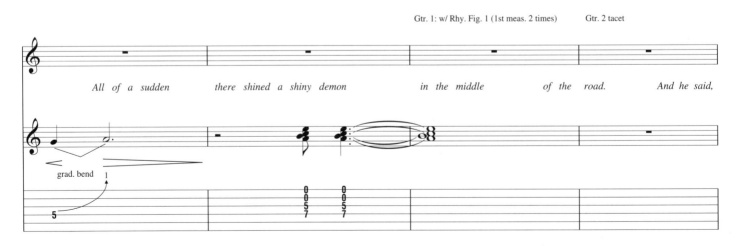

Sung: "Play the best song in the world __ or I'll eat your souls." __

Gtr. 1: w/ Rhy. Fig. 1 (2 times)

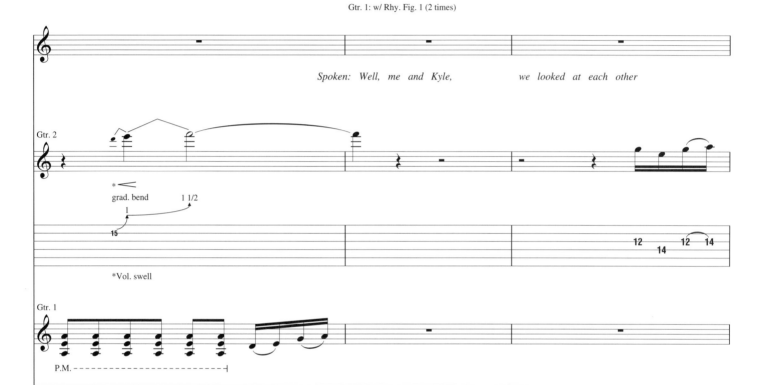

Spoken: Well, me and Kyle, we looked at each other

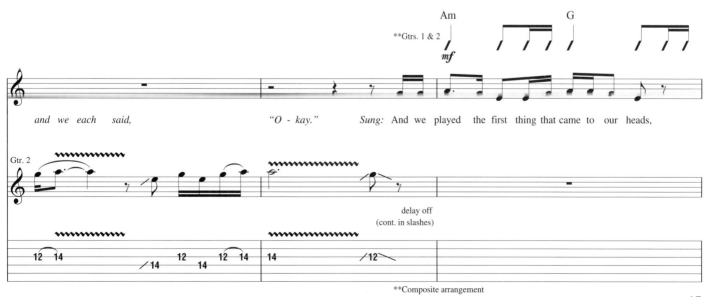

and we each said, "O - kay." Sung: And we played the first thing that came to our heads,

**Composite arrangement

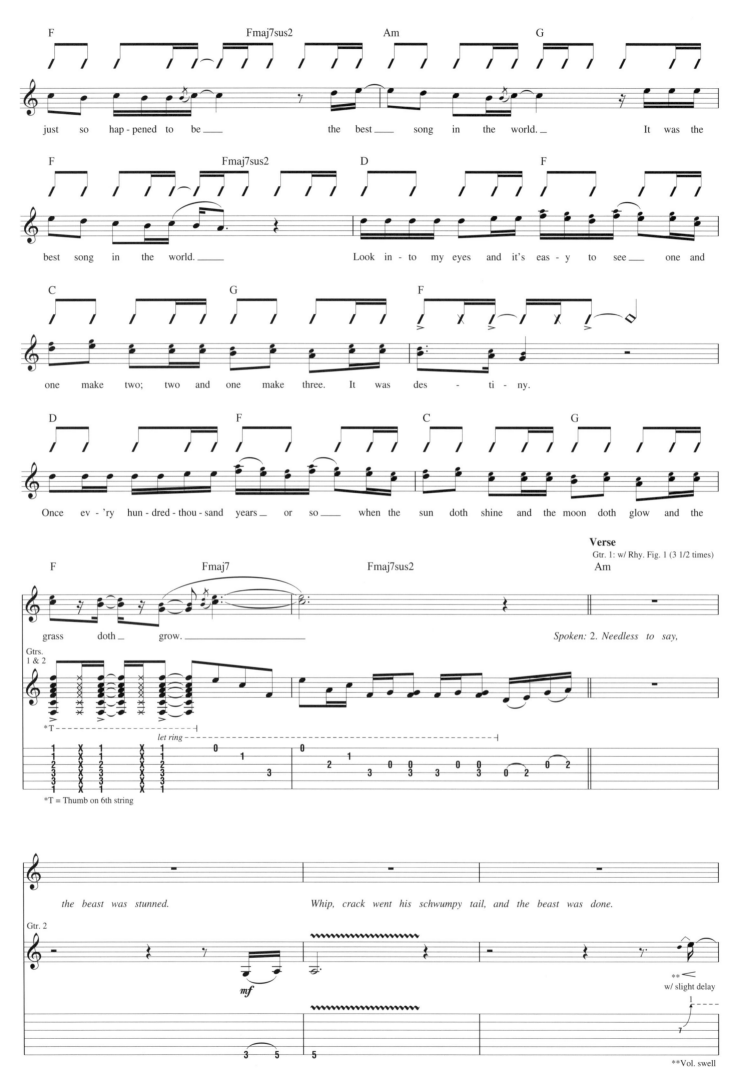

just so hap-pened to be ___ the best ___ song in the world. ___ It was the

best song in the world. ___ Look in-to my eyes and it's eas-y to see ___ one and

one make two; two and one make three. It was des- ti - ny.

Once ev- 'ry hun-dred-thou-sand years ___ or so ___ when the sun doth shine and the moon doth glow and the

Verse
Gtr. 1: w/ Rhy. Fig. 1 (3 1/2 times)

grass doth ___ grow. _____

Spoken: 2. Needless to say,

Gtrs.
1 & 2

*T -
let ring -

*T = Thumb on 6th string

the beast was stunned.

Whip, crack went his schwumpy tail, and the beast was done.

Gtr. 2

mf

** <
w/ slight delay

**Vol. swell

Could - n't re - mem - ber _____ the great - est song _ in the world, _____ yeah, _ oh, _____ no. This is a trib -

Chorus

ute, _____ oh, _____ to the great - est song in _____ the world, al - right. _____

Gtrs. 1 & 2: w/ Rhy. Fig. 2 (2 times)

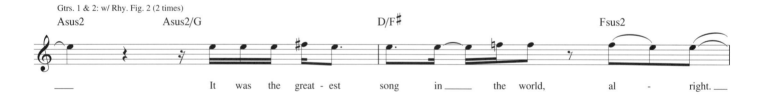

_____ It was the great - est song in _____ the world, al - right. _____

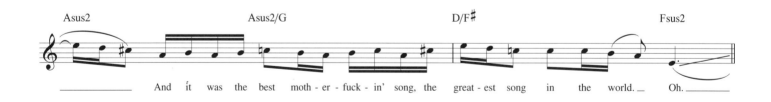

_____ And it was the best moth - er - fuck - in' song, the great - est song in the world. _ Oh. _____

Interlude

Gtr. 1 tacet

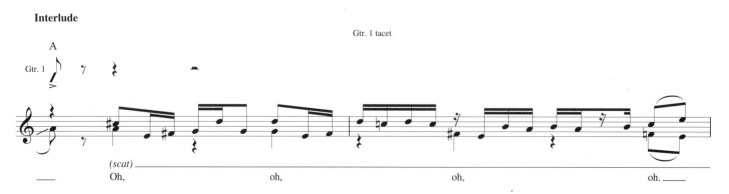

(scat) _____
_ Oh, oh, oh, oh. _____

(scat) _____
Oh,   oh,   oh,   oh,   oh,   oh,   oh,   oh.

Gtr. 2

w/ dist.

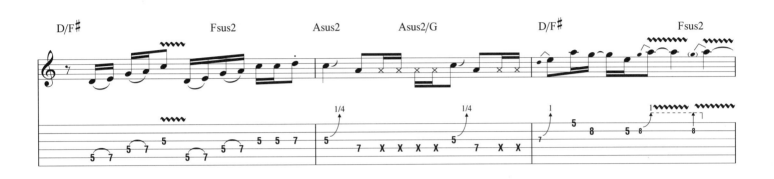

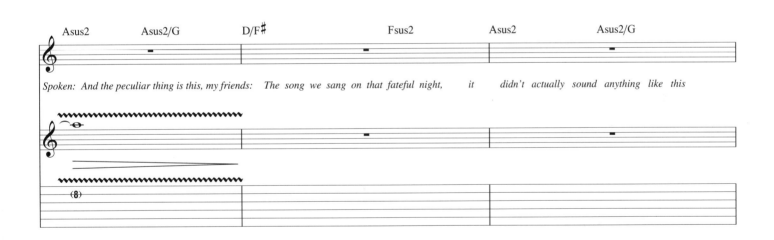

Spoken: And the peculiar thing is this, my friends: The song we sang on that fateful night,   it   didn't actually sound anything like this

Chorus

Gtr. 1: w/ Rhy. Fig. 2 (4 times)

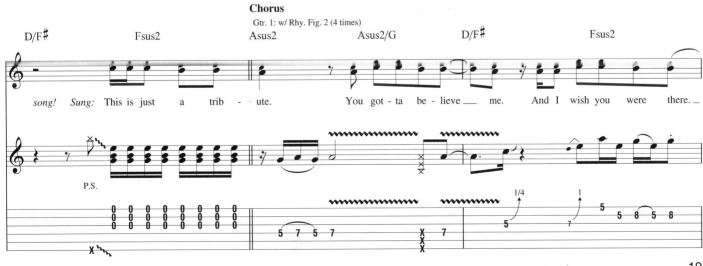

song! Sung: This is just a trib - ute.   You got-ta be-lieve___ me.   And I wish you were there.___

P.S.

19

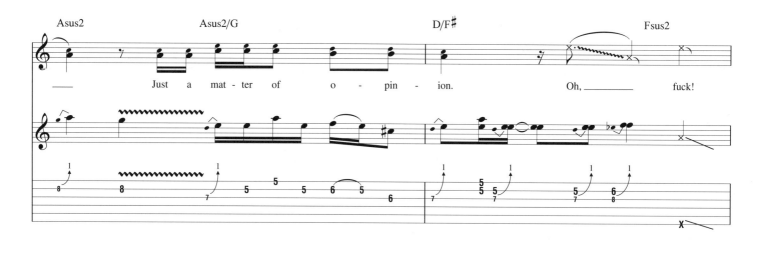

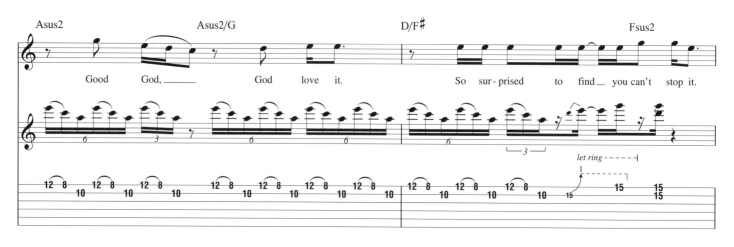

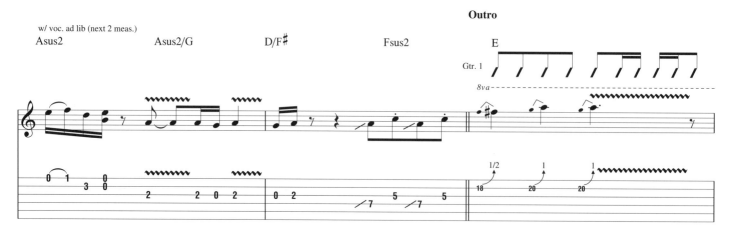

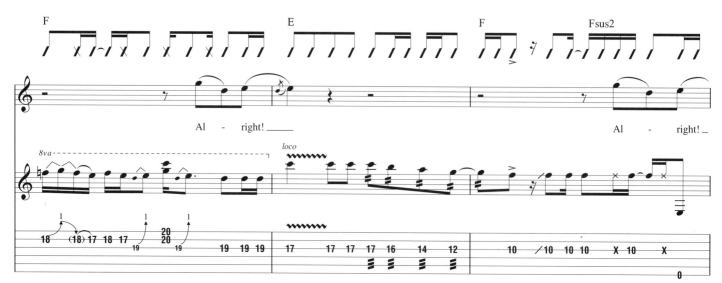

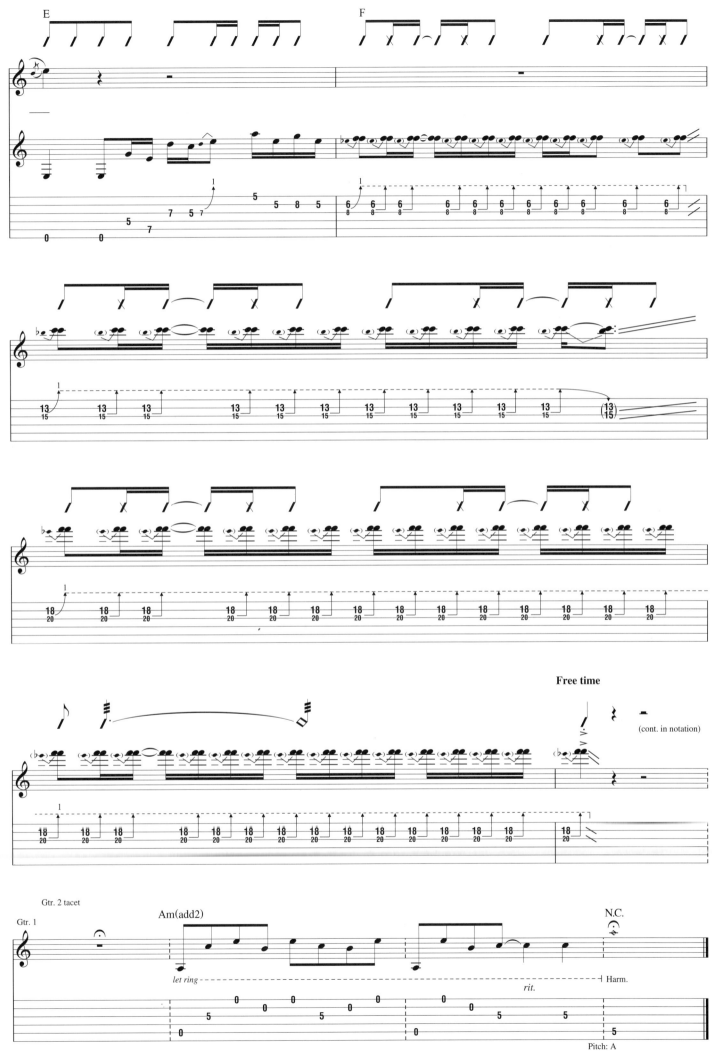

WONDERBOY

Words and Music by
Jack Black and Kyle Gass

Sung: 3. His - to - ry of Won - der - boy and young __

Nas - ty - man. __ Rig - gah - goo - goo, rig - gah - goo - goo. A se - cret to be told, __ a

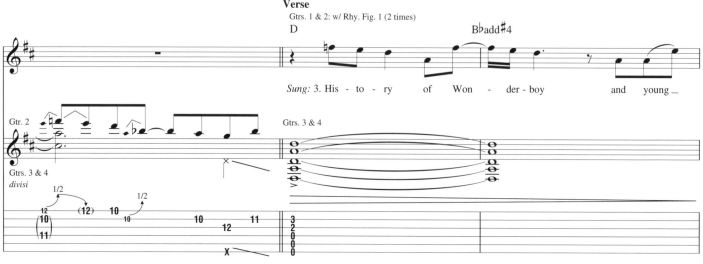

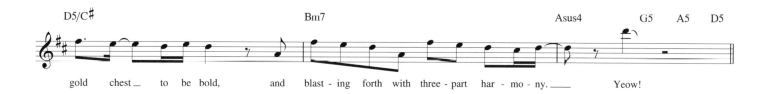
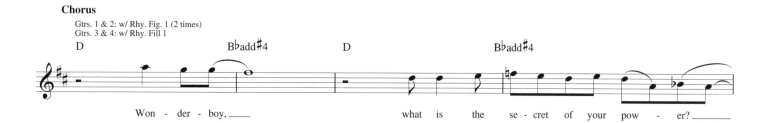

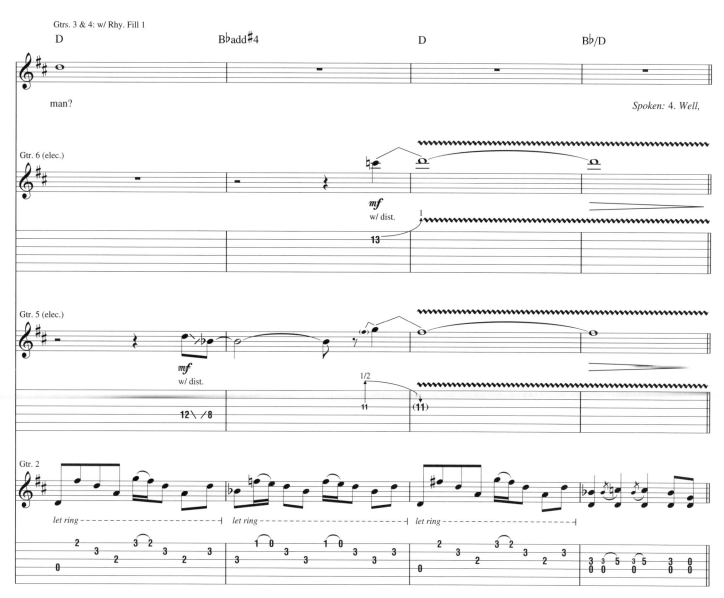

FUCK HER GENTLY

Words and Music by
Jack Black and Kyle Gass

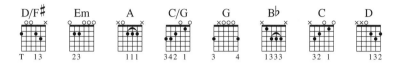

Intro
Moderately ♩ = 120

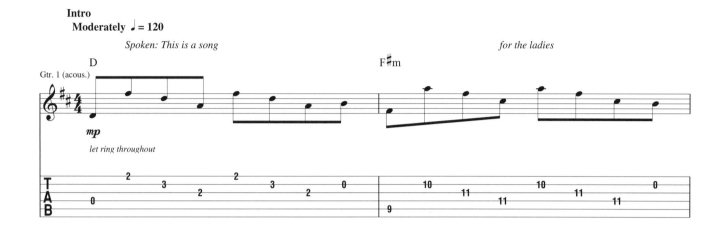

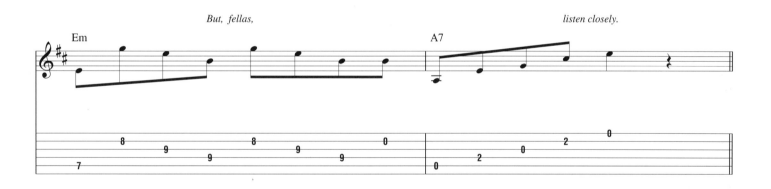

Verse

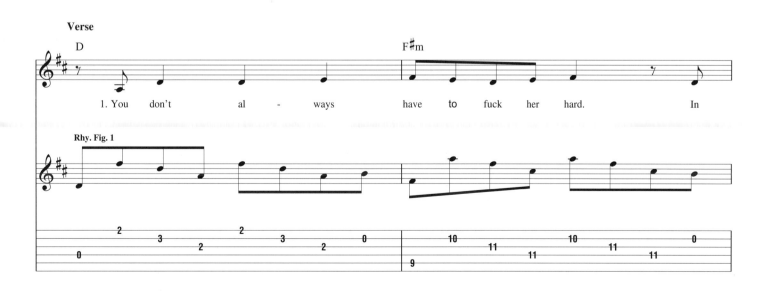

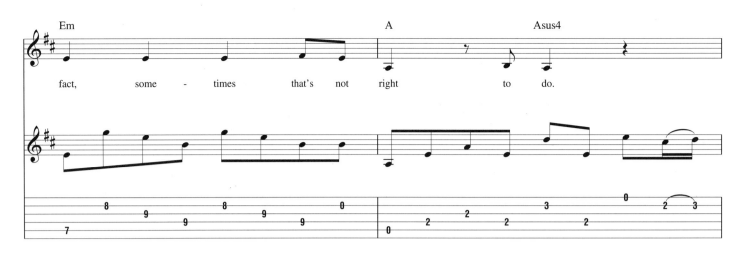

fact, some - times that's not right to do.

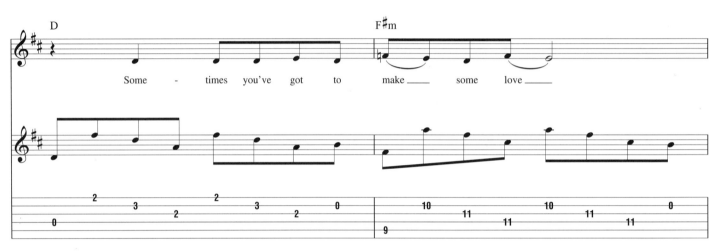

Some - times you've got to make ___ some love ___

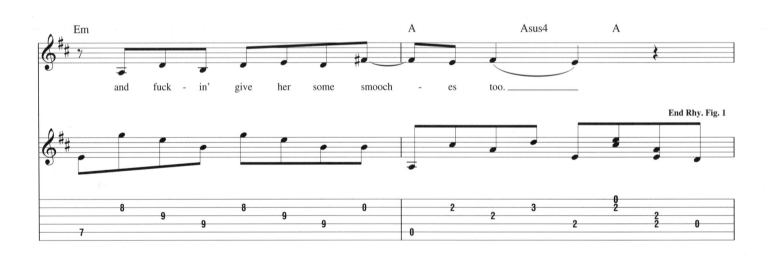

and fuck - in' give her some smooch - es too. ___

End Rhy. Fig. 1

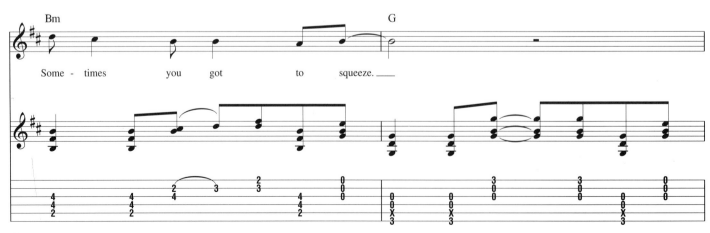

Some - times you got to squeeze. ___

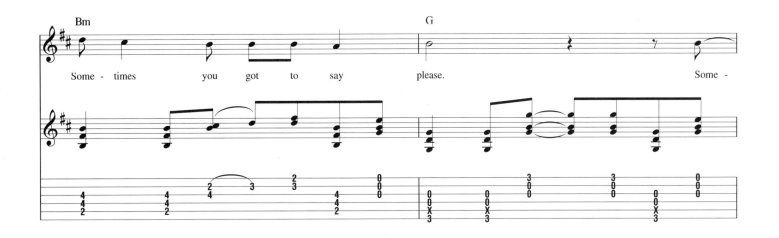

Some - times   you   got   to   say   please.   Some -

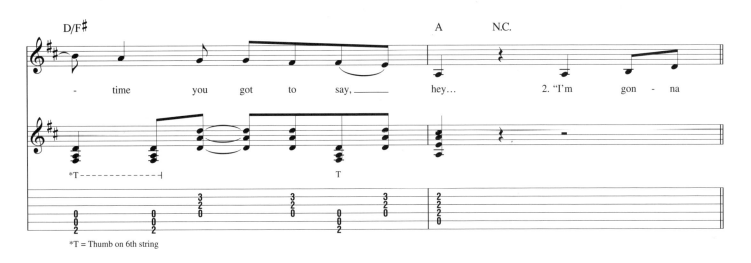

- time   you   got   to   say,_____   hey…   2. "I'm   gon - na

*T = Thumb on 6th string

Verse

Gtr. 1: w/ Rhy. Fig. 1

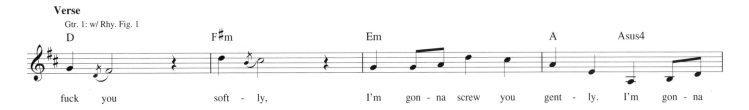

fuck   you   soft - ly,   I'm   gon - na   screw   you   gent - ly.   I'm   gon - na

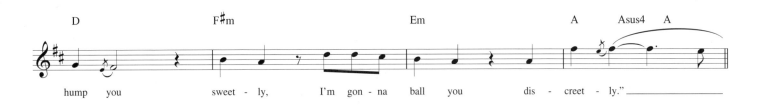

hump   you   sweet - ly,   I'm   gon - na   ball   you   dis - creet - ly."_____

Chorus

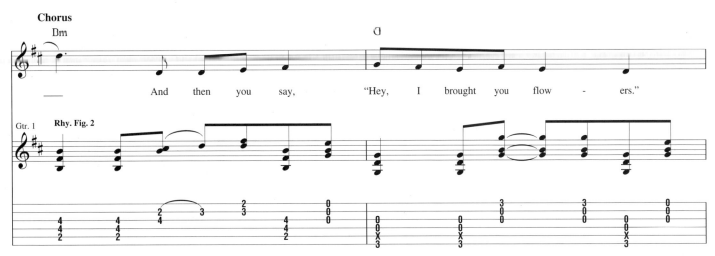

And   then   you   say,   "Hey,   I   brought   you   flow - ers."

Gtr. 1   **Rhy. Fig. 2**

EXPLOSIVO

Words and Music by
Jack Black and Kyle Gass

34

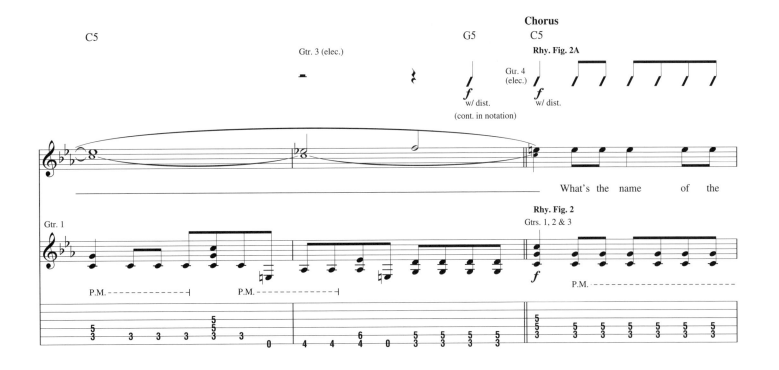

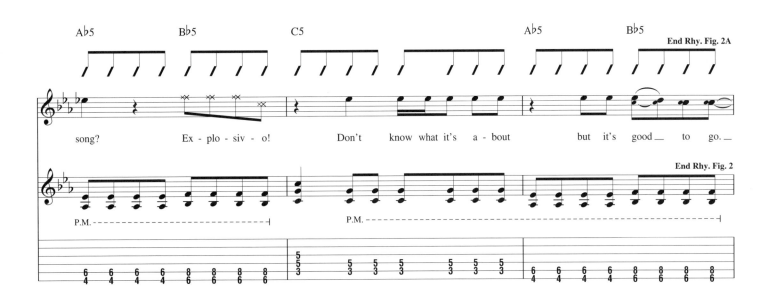

DIO

Words and Music by
Jack Black and Kyle Gass

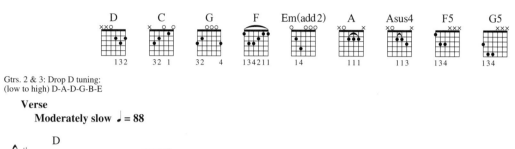

Gtrs. 2 & 3: Drop D tuning:
(low to high) D-A-D-G-B-E

Verse

Moderately slow ♩ = 88

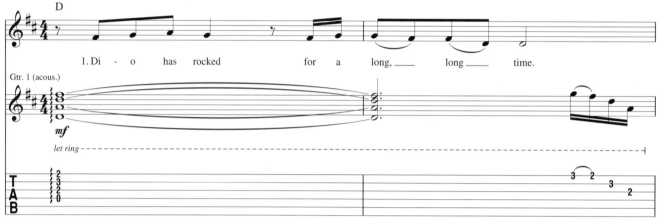

1. Di - o has rocked for a long, ____ long ____ time.

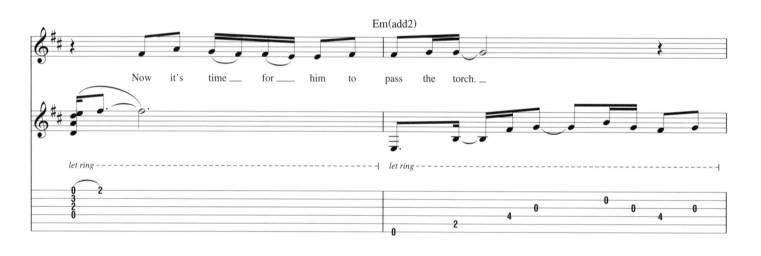

Now it's time ____ for ____ him to pass the torch. ____

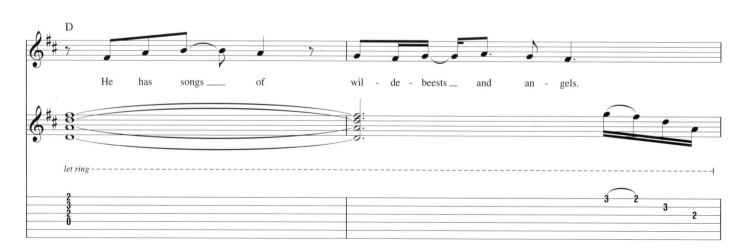

He has songs ____ of wil - de - beests ____ and an - gels.

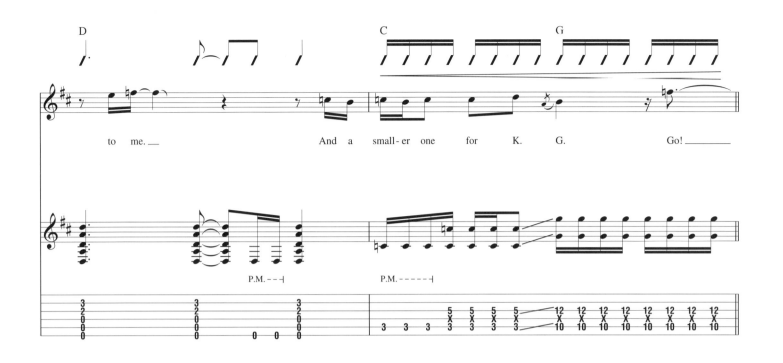

to me. ___   And a small-er one for K. G.   Go! ___

Outro-Guitar Solo

___   Go! ___   Di - o! ___   Di - o! ___

(cont. in notation)

Gtr. 3
(elec.)

f
w/ dist.

Rhy. Fig. 1

Gtr. 2

End Rhy. Fig. 1

P.M. ---   P.M.   P.M. ---   P.M. ---   P.M. ----------   P.M. ---

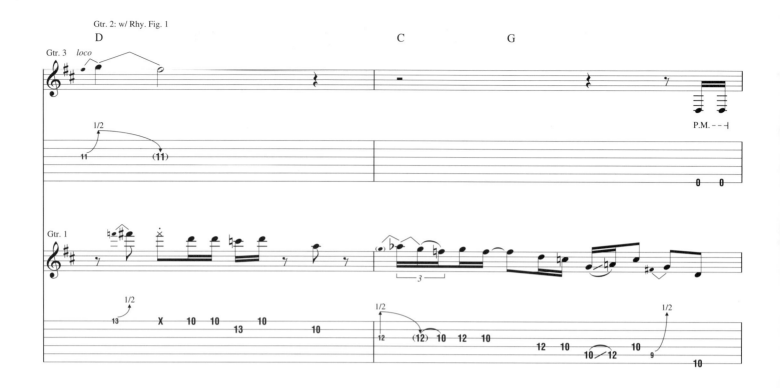

KYLE QUIT THE BAND

Words and Music by
Jack Black and Kyle Gass

And ev -'ry - one, you're all in - vit - ed to the bash, _____

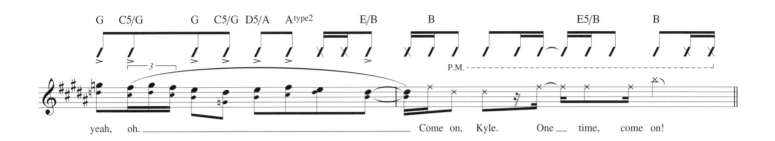

yeah, oh. _____ Come on, Kyle. One ___ time, come on!

Guitar Solo

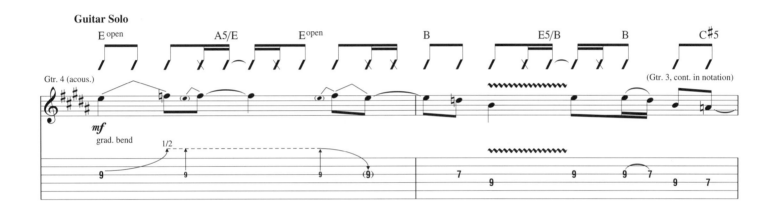

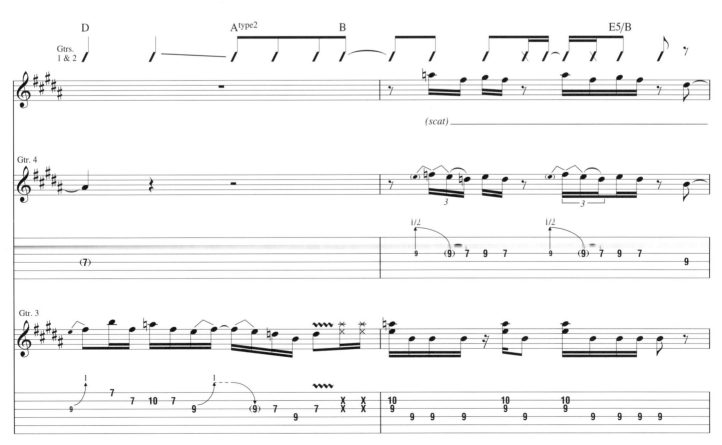

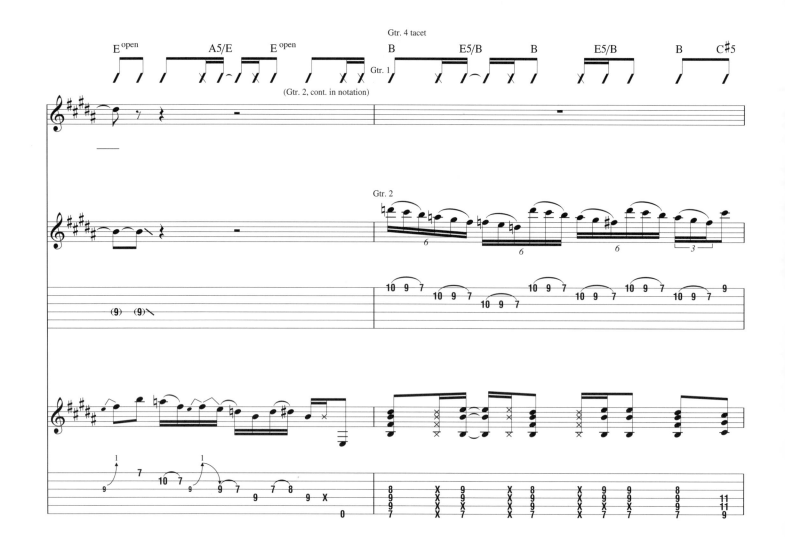

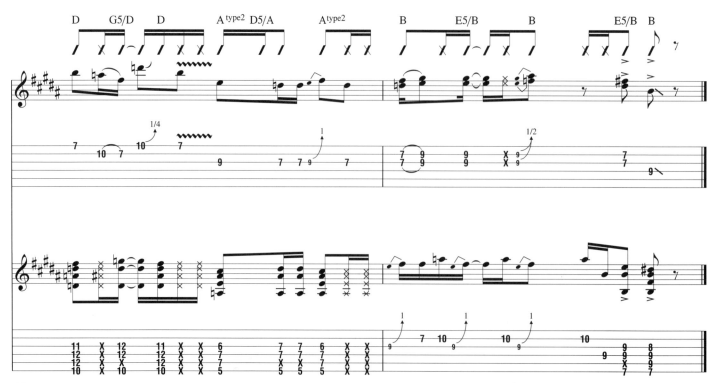

THE ROAD

48

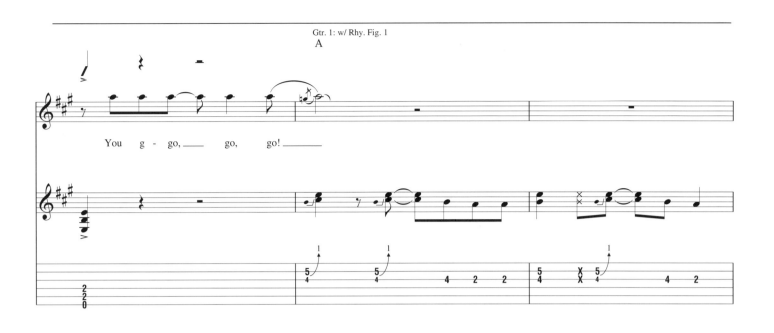

You g - go, ___ go, go! ___

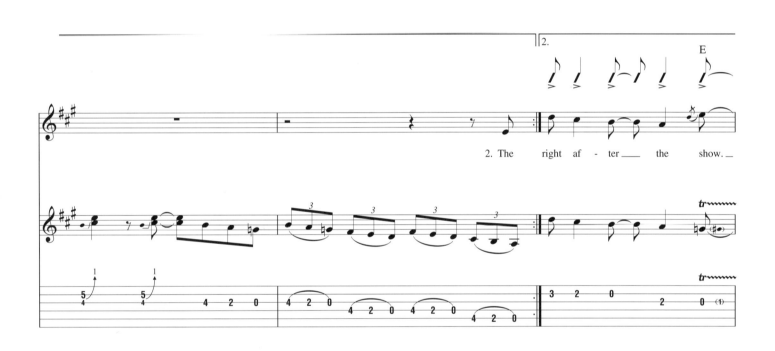

2. The right af - ter ___ the show. ___

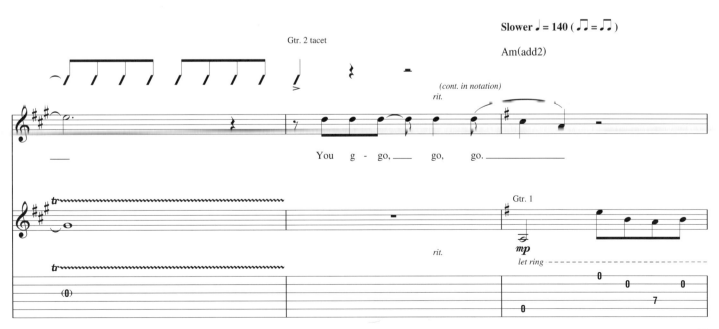

You g - go, ___ go, go. ___

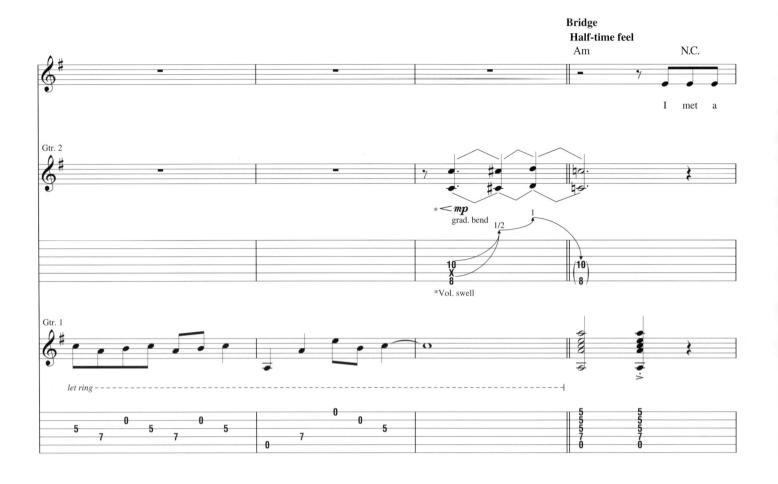

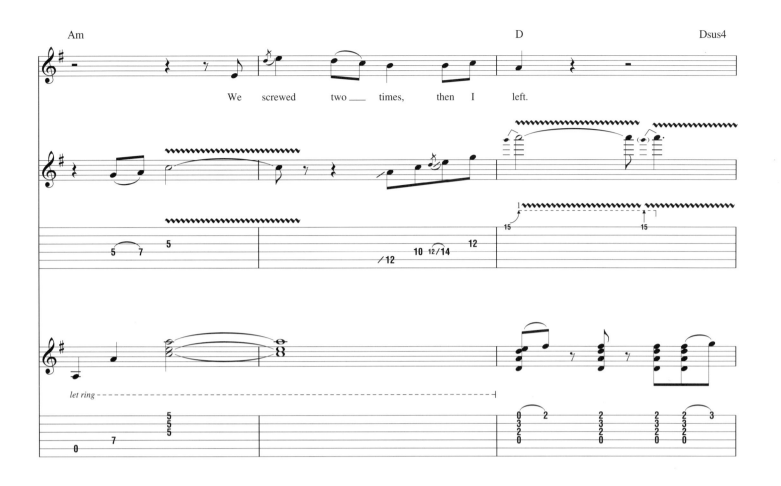

We screwed two ___ times, then I left.

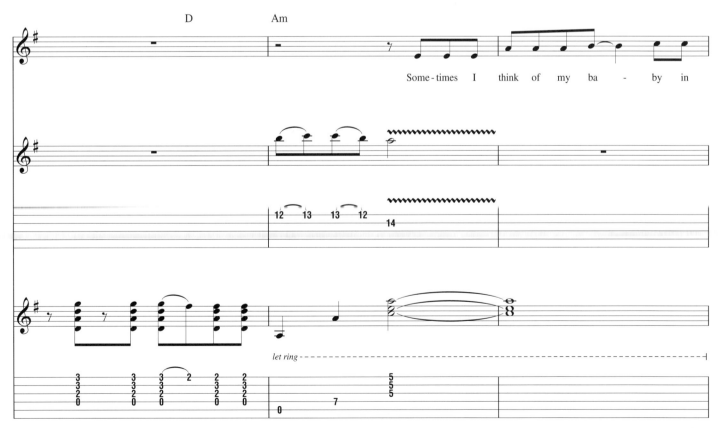

Some-times I think of my ba - by in

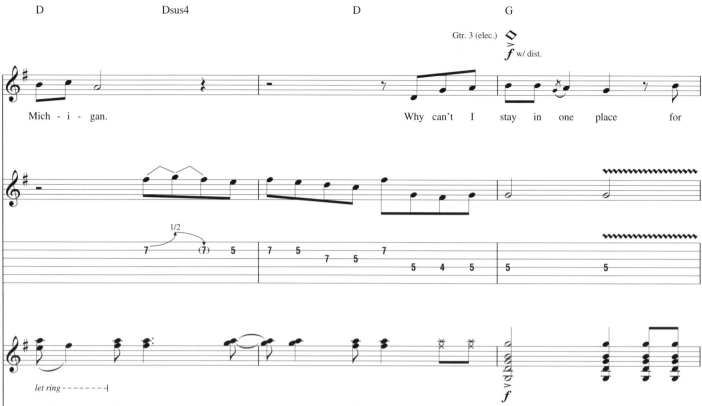

Mich - i - gan.   Why can't I stay in one place for

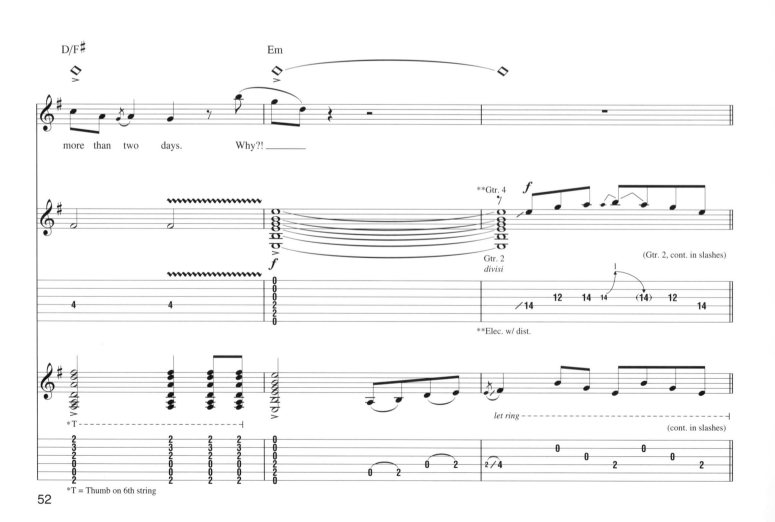

more than two days.   Why?! _____

*T = Thumb on 6th string

52

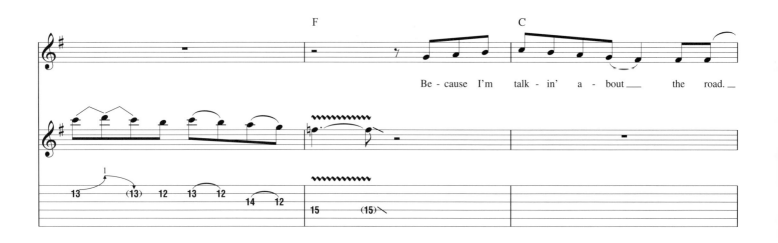

Be - cause I'm talk - in' a - bout ___ the road. __

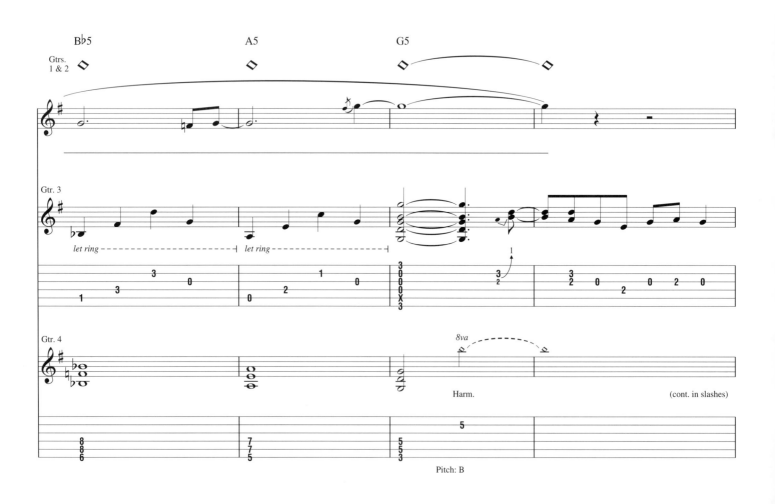

Harm.

(cont. in slashes)

Pitch: B

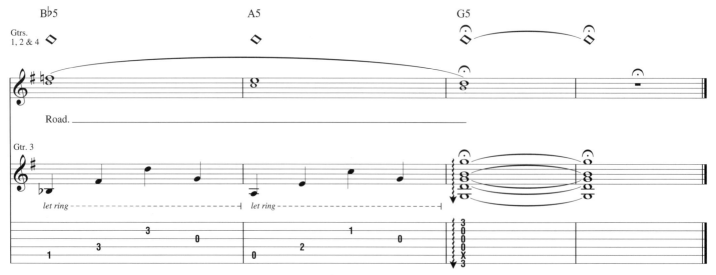

Road. _____

54

LEE

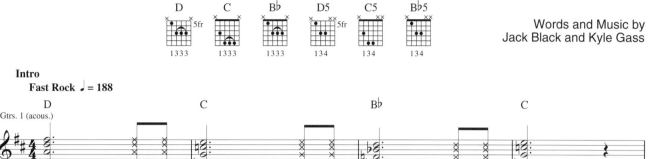

Words and Music by
Jack Black and Kyle Gass

Intro
Fast Rock ♩ = 188

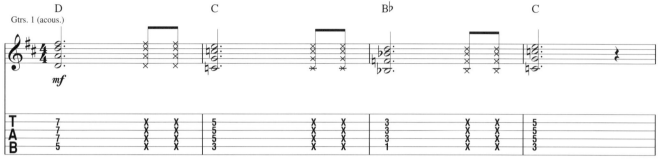

**Composite arrangement; Gtr. 2 (elec. w/ dist.) played *mf*

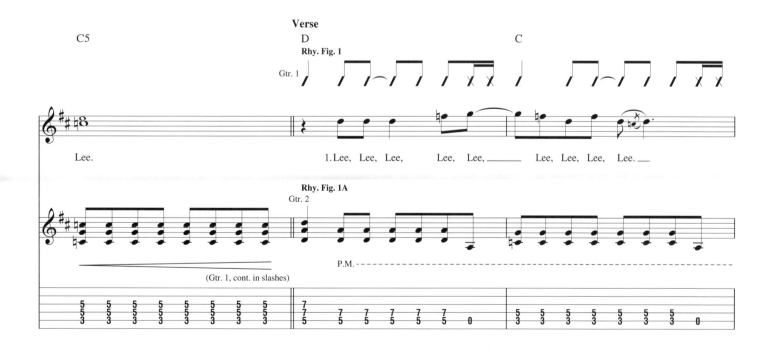

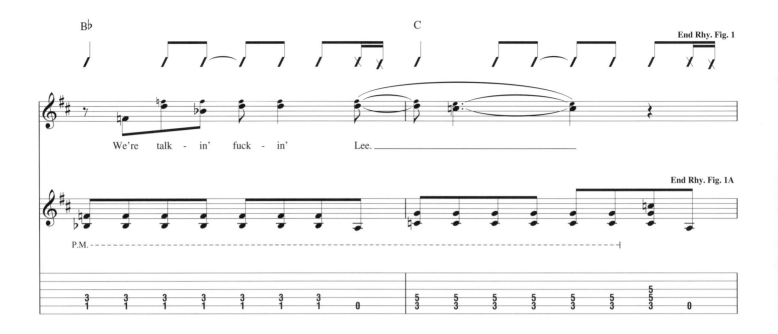

Lyrics: We're talk-in' fuck-in' Lee.

Gtr. 1: w/ Rhy. Fig. 1 (3 times)
Gtr. 2: w/ Rhy. Fig. 1A (2 times)

Lyrics: I had a friend named Lee. He cast a spell, a spell

Lyrics: on me. If me and Lee and K. G. could be free,

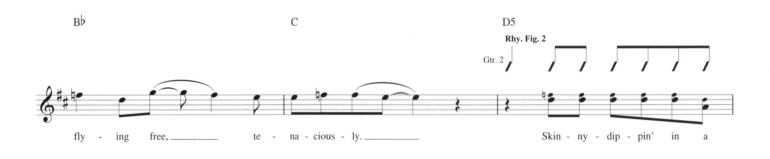

Lyrics: fly-ing free, te-na-cious-ly. Skin-ny-dip-pin' in a

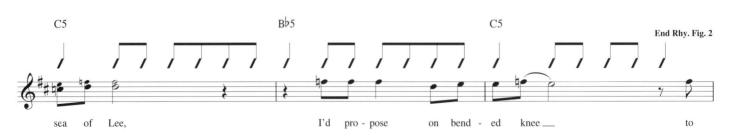

Lyrics: sea of Lee, I'd pro-pose on bend-ed knee to

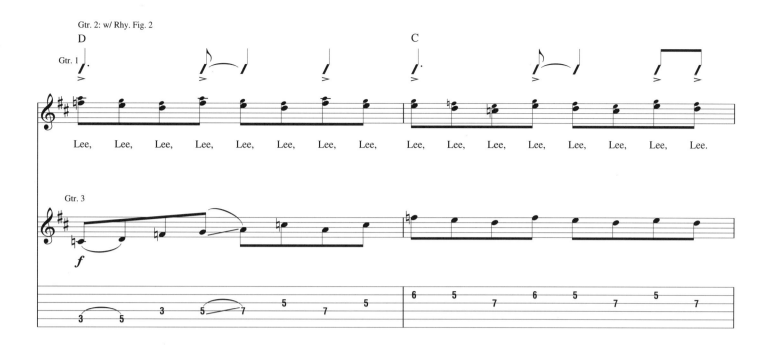

Lee, Lee, Lee, Lee, Lee, Lee, Lee, Lee, Lee, Lee, Lee, Lee, Lee, Lee, Lee, Lee.

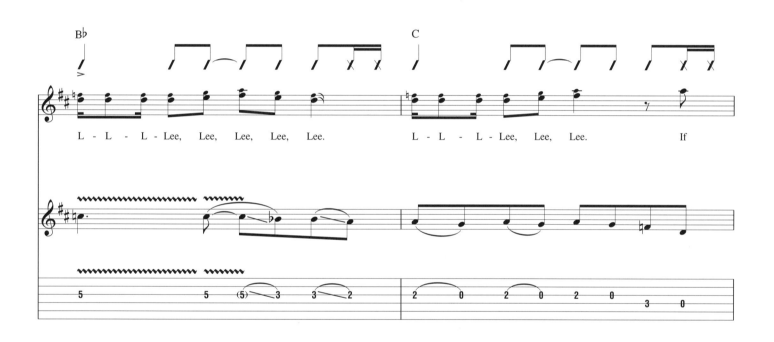

L - L - L - Lee, Lee, Lee, Lee, Lee.   L - L - L - Lee, Lee, Lee.   If

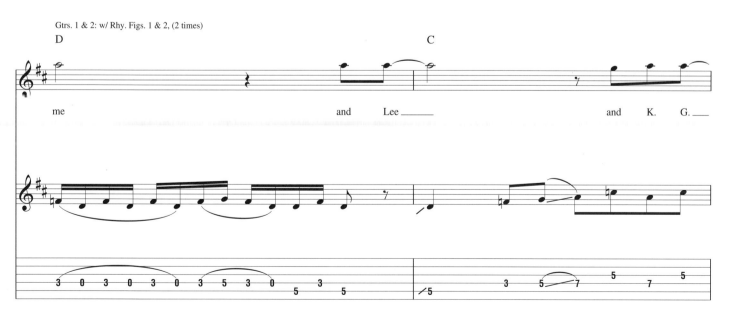

me   and   Lee   and   K.   G.

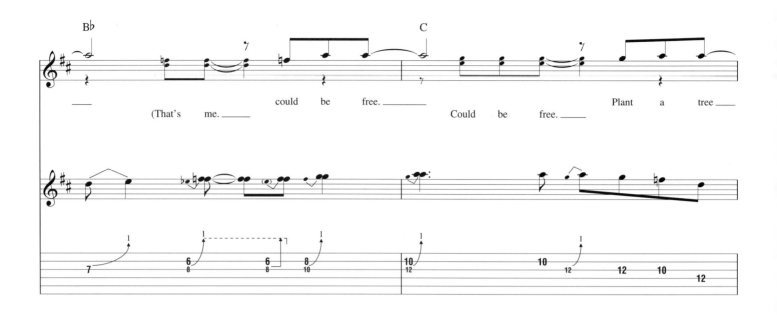

could be free. _____ Could be free. _____ Plant a tree _____

(That's me. _____

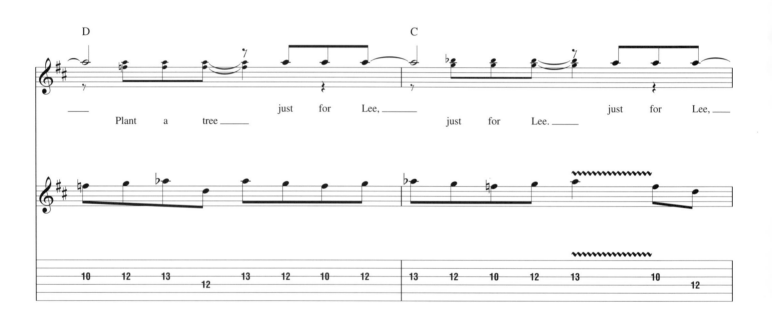

Plant a tree _____ just for Lee, _____ just for Lee. _____ just for Lee, _____

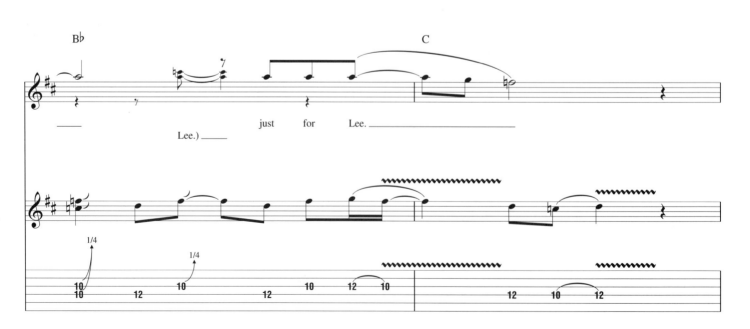

just for Lee. _____

Lee.) _____

FRIENDSHIP

Words and Music by
Jack Black and Kyle Gass

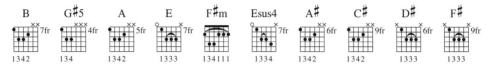

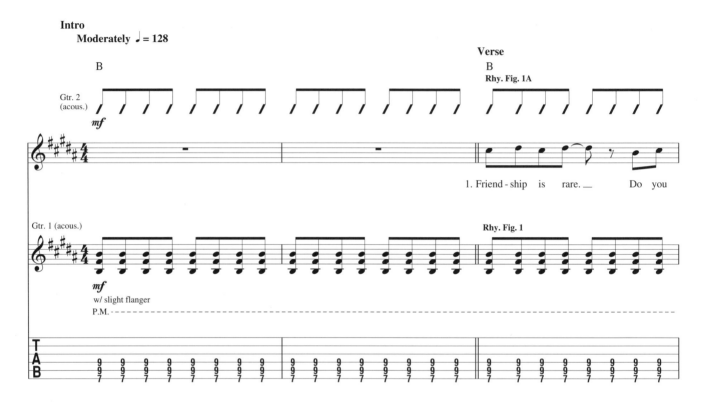

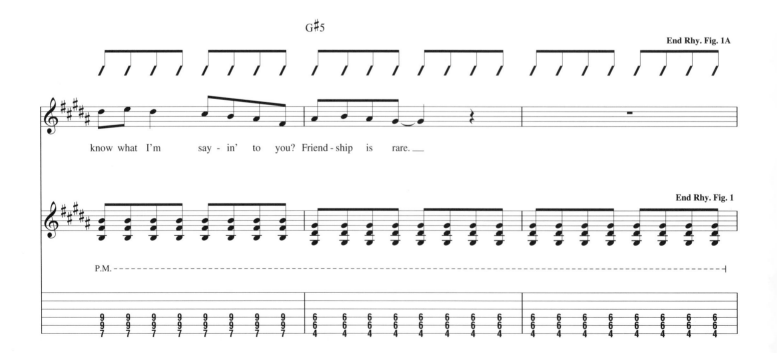

My der - ri - ére, _____ when you find out much lat - er that they

G#5

don't real - ly care. _____ It's

Chorus

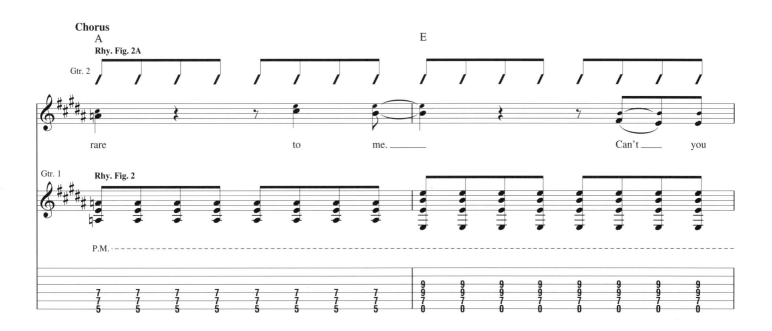

rare to me. _____ Can't _____ you

rare to me. _____ Can't _____ you

see? _____ It's

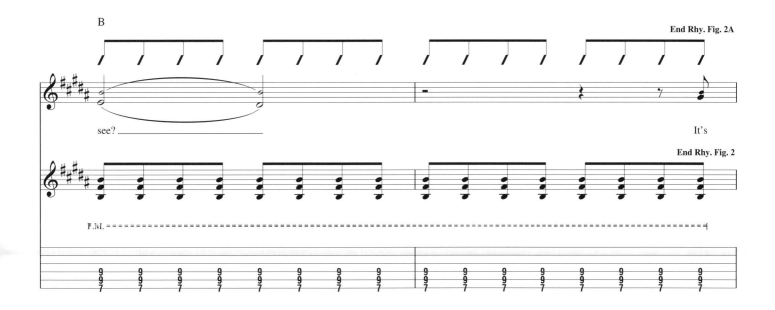

Gtrs. 1 & 2: w/ Rhy. Figs. 2 & 2A

A **E** **B**

rare to me. _____ Can't you see? _____ 2. Oh,

Verse

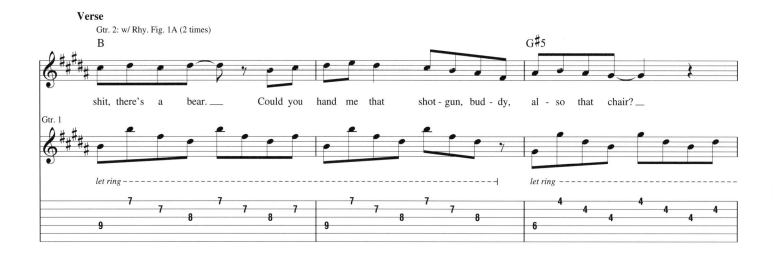

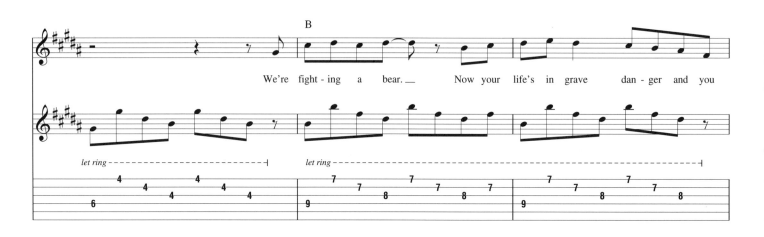

Chorus

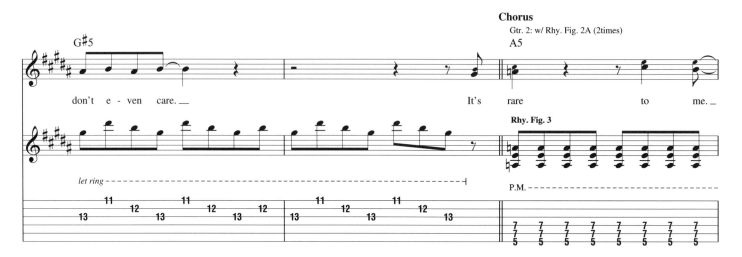

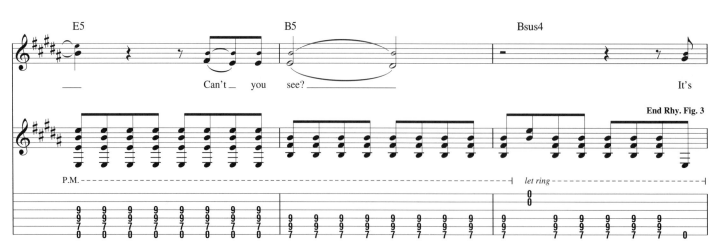

KARATE

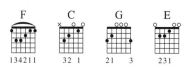

Words and Music by
Jack Black and Kyle Gass

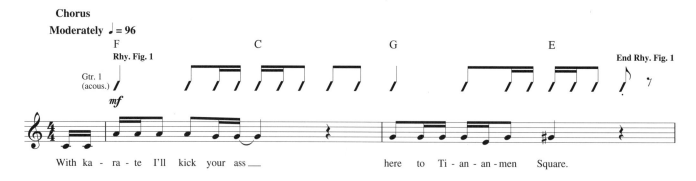

With ka-ra-te I'll kick your ass ___ here to Ti-an-an-men Square.

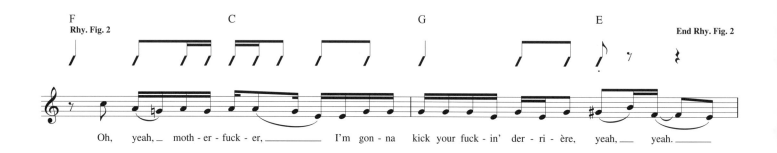

Oh, yeah, _ moth-er-fuck-er, _____ I'm gon-na kick your fuck-in' der-ri-ère, yeah, _ yeah. ___

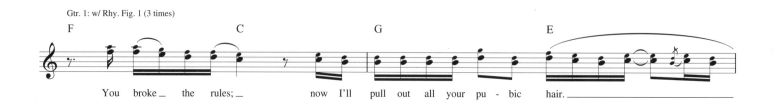

You broke _ the rules; _ now I'll pull out all your pu-bic hair. _____

_ You moth-er-fuck-er. ___

You moth-er-fuck-er. ___

Ky-le be-trayed me and then he lied, tried to hide. And I died deep in-side and you know the rea-son why.

Chorus

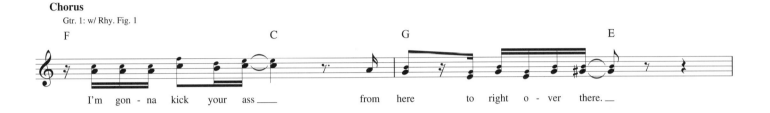

Gtr. 1: w/ Rhy. Fig. 1

I'm gon-na kick your ass ____ from here to right o-ver there. ____

Gtr. 1: w/ Rhy. Fig. 2

Oh, yeah, ____ moth-er-fuck-er, _____ I'm gon-na kick your fuck-in' der-ri-ère, yeah, ____ yeah. ____

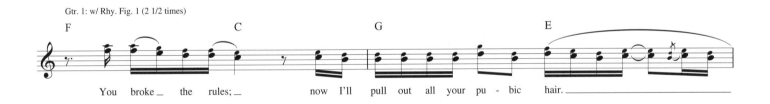

Gtr. 1: w/ Rhy. Fig. 1 (2 1/2 times)

You broke __ the rules; __ now I'll pull out all your pu-bic hair. ____

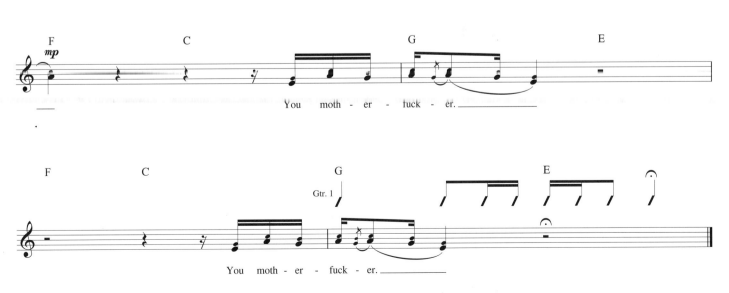

You moth-er-fuck-er. ____

Gtr. 1

You moth-er-fuck-er. ____

ROCK YOUR SOCKS

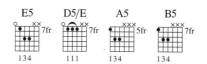

Words and Music by
Jack Black and Kyle Gass

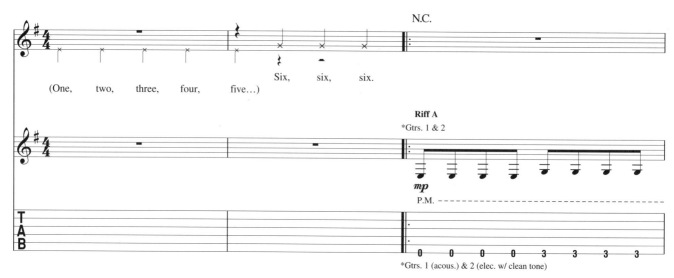

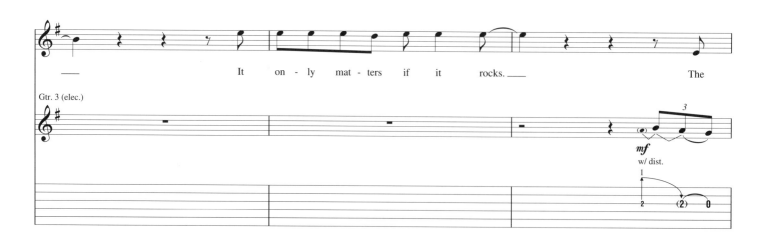

main thing that we do ____ is to rock your socks ____ off.

There's no such thing as a rock prod - i - gy,

'cause rock - and - roll is bo - gus. Right, ___ K. G.?

(Right!)

On - ly thing that real - ly

mat - ters is a clas - si - cal sauce. ____

And

Gtr. 3 tacet

Gtr. 2

P.M.

P.M.

grad. bend

that's why me and K. G. ___ are clas - si - c'lly trained to rock your fuck - in' socks ___

Gtr. 3

Gtr. 2

semi-harm. -

P.M. - - -

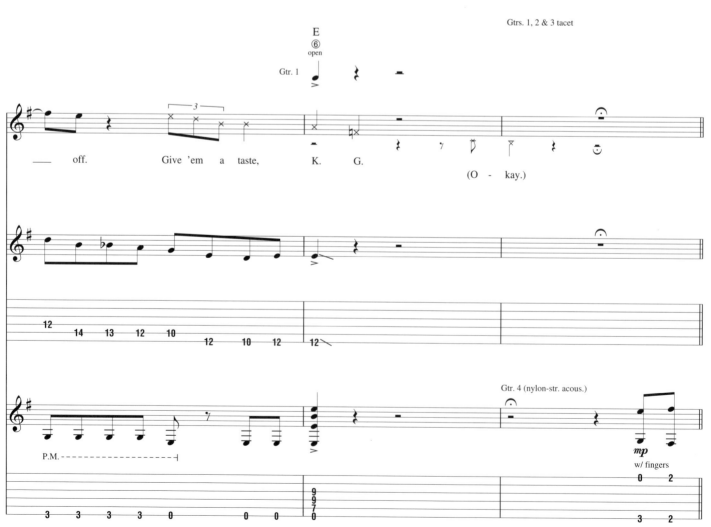

Gtrs. 1, 2 & 3 tacet

E
⑥
open

Gtr. 1

___ off. Give 'em a taste, K. G.

(O - kay.)

Gtr. 4 (nylon-str. acous.)

P.M. - - - - - - - - - - - - - - - - -

mp
w/ fingers

Chorus

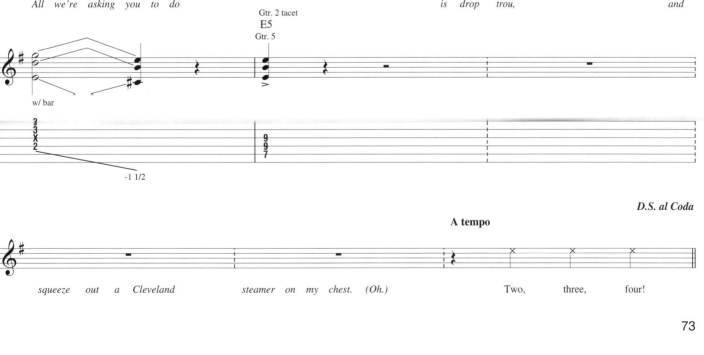

DOUBLE TEAM

Words and Music by
Jack Black and Kyle Gass

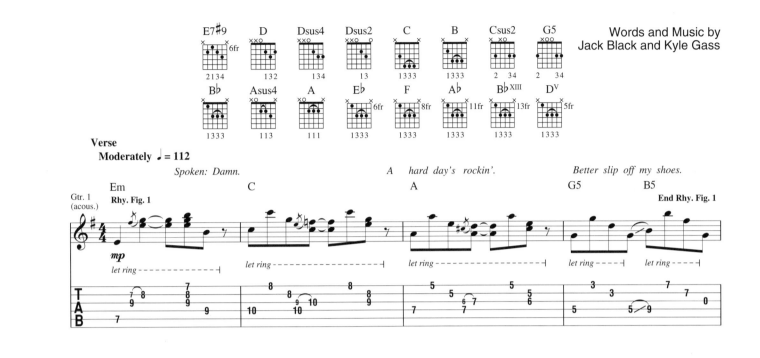

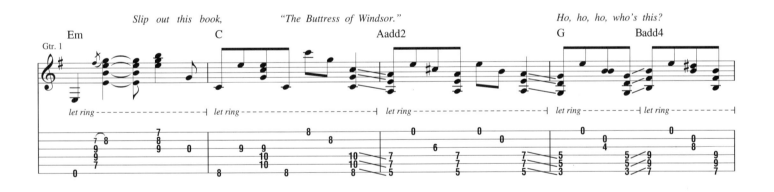

Gtr. 1: w/ Rhy. Fig. 2 (3 times)

Em — Cmaj7 — Aadd2

Listen, honey. Sung: Think - in' 'bout a cou - ple things to say to you. ___

G — Badd4 — Em — Cmaj7 — Aadd2

Spoken: Showin'. Growin'. Man, I'd like to place my hand upon your fuckin' sexy ass and squeeze.

G — Badd4 — Em — Cmaj7

Sung: And squeeze. ___ Take off ___ your blouse ___ and your un - der - pants. ___

Chorus

A5 — G5 — B5 — E5 — N.C.

___ Then take a ___ look, ___ 'cause here me and K. G. come na - ked out

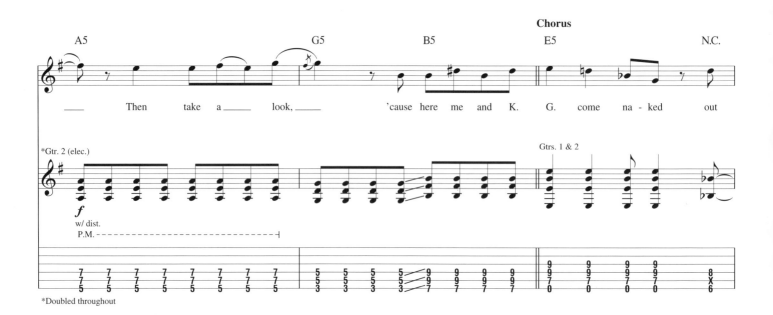

*Gtr. 2 (elec.)

Gtrs. 1 & 2

f

w/ dist.

P.M. ----------------------

*Doubled throughout

E5 — N.C.

of the side hatch with the o - ils and per - fume and in - cense.

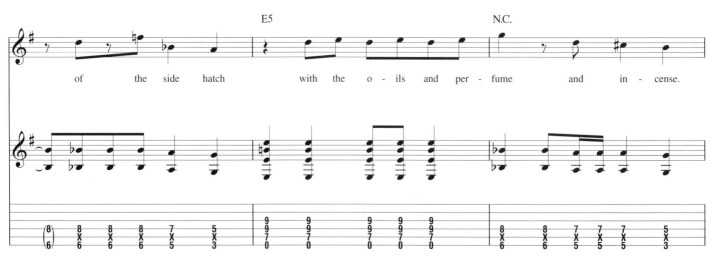

___ likes to cream jeans. Have you ev-er been worked ___ on by

(Sex.) ___

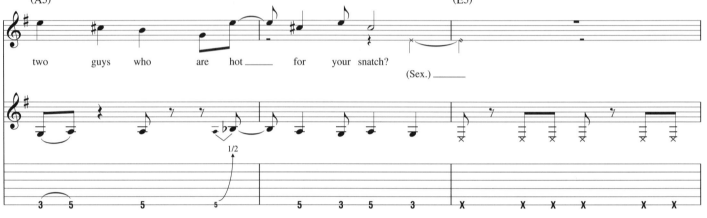

two guys who are hot ___ for your snatch?

(Sex.) ___

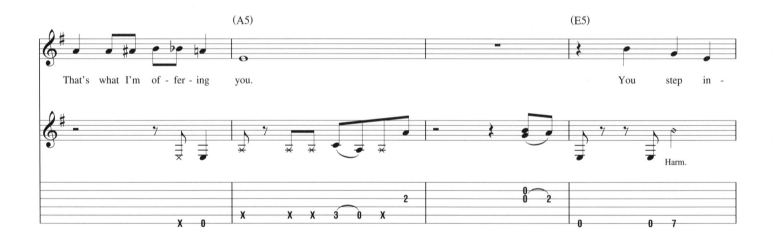

That's what I'm of-fer-ing you. You step in -

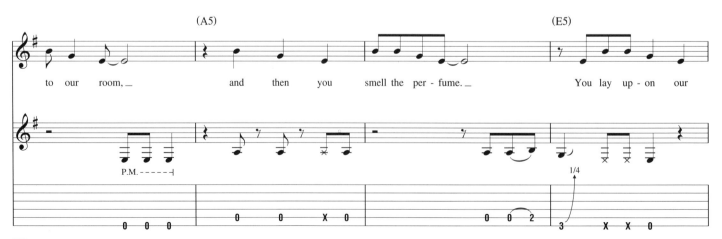

to our room, ___ and then you smell the per-fume. ___ You lay up-on our

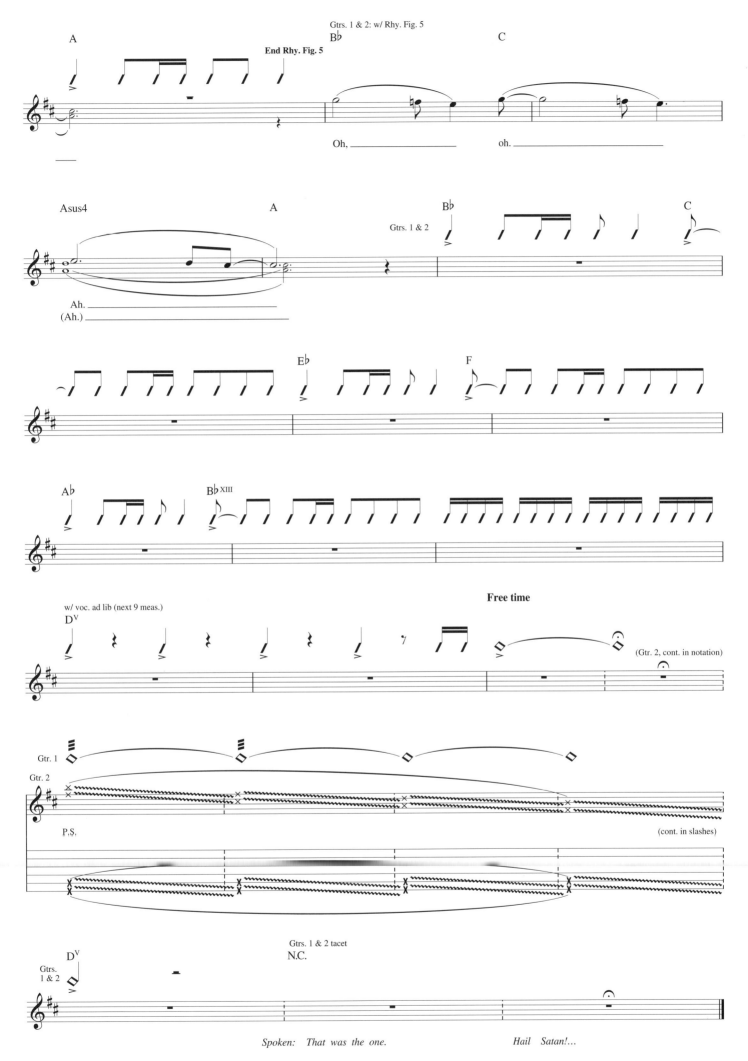

Oh, _____ oh. _____

Ah. _____
(Ah.) _____

w/ voc. ad lib (next 9 meas.)

Free time

(Gtr. 2, cont. in notation)

Gtr. 1

Gtr. 2

P.S.   (cont. in slashes)

Gtrs. 1 & 2 tacet
N.C.

Gtrs. 1 & 2

Spoken: That was the one.   *Hail Satan!...*

CITY HALL

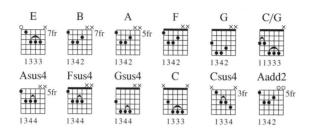

Words and Music by
Jack Black and Kyle Gass

Intro
Moderately slow ♩ = 96

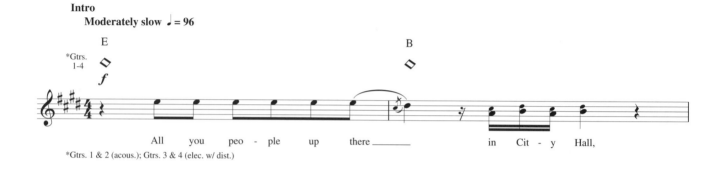

All you peo - ple up there _____ in Cit - y Hall,

*Gtrs. 1 & 2 (acous.); Gtrs. 3 & 4 (elec. w/ dist.)

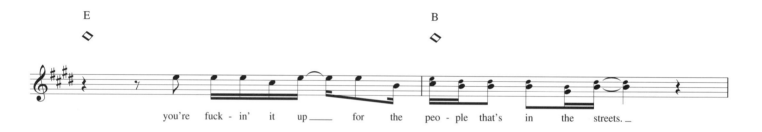

you're fuck - in' it up _____ for the peo - ple that's in the streets. _____

(cont. in notation)

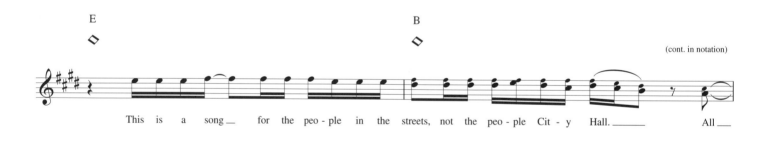

This is a song _____ for the peo - ple in the streets, not the peo - ple Cit - y Hall. _____ All _____

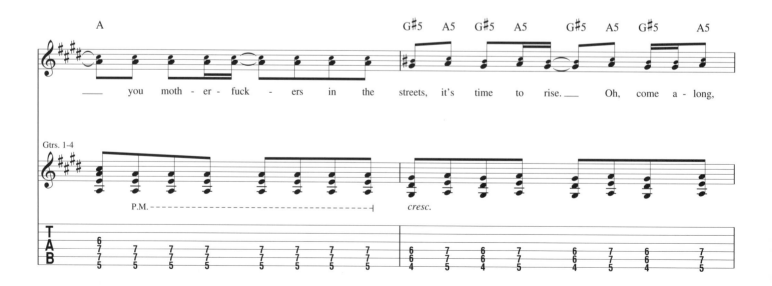

_____ you moth - er - fuck - ers in the streets, it's time to rise. _____ Oh, come a - long,

Gtrs. 1-4

P.M. -| cresc.

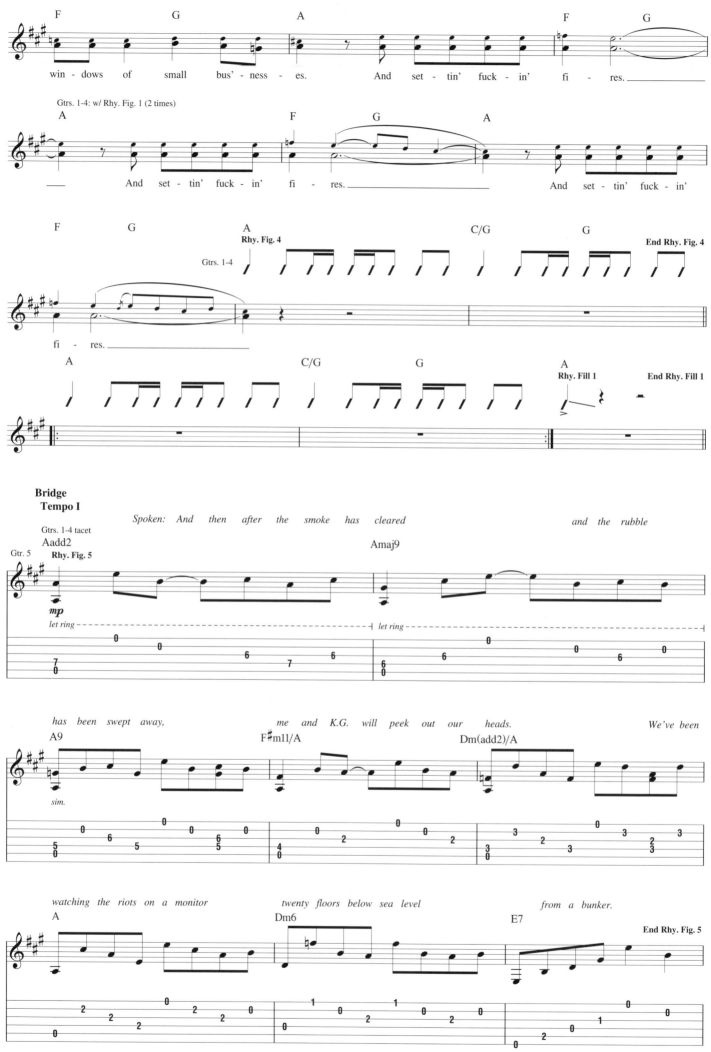

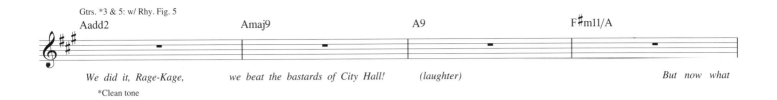

Gtrs. *3 & 5: w/ Rhy. Fig. 5

Aadd2   Amaj9   A9   F#m11/A

We did it, Rage-Kage,   *we beat the bastards of City Hall!*   *(laughter)*   *But now what*

*Clean tone

Dm(add2)/A   A   Dm6   E7

will we do?   *We must rebuild.*   *But who will lead us in the rebuilding process?*   *Man, it's got to*

be someone with the know-how   *and the elbow grease*   *to lead us to a new land.*

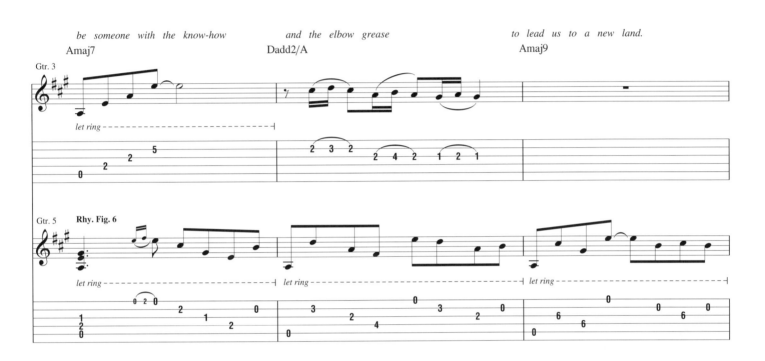

Gtr. 3

Amaj7   Dadd2/A   Amaj9

Gtr. 5   **Rhy. Fig. 6**

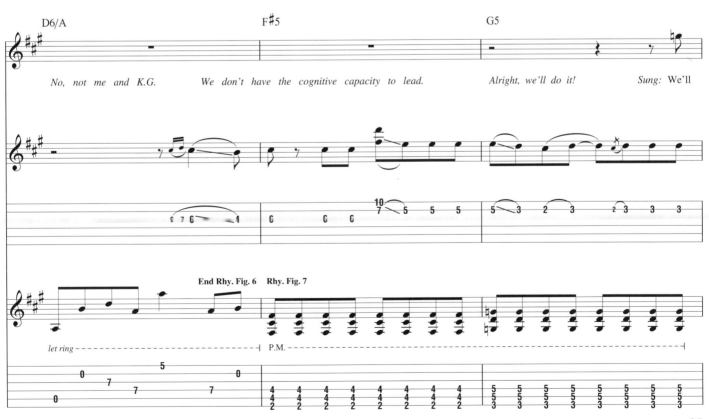

D6/A   F#5   G5

No, not me and K.G.   *We don't have the cognitive capacity to lead.*   *Alright, we'll do it!*   *Sung: We'll*

End Rhy. Fig. 6   **Rhy. Fig. 7**

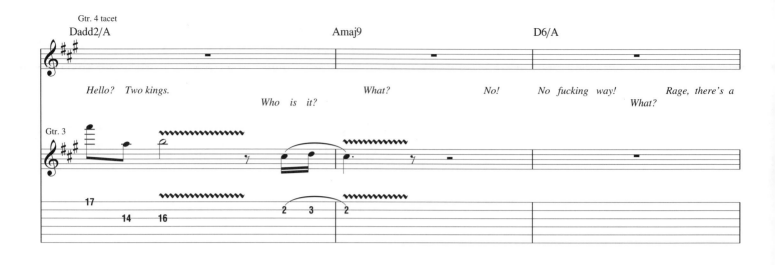

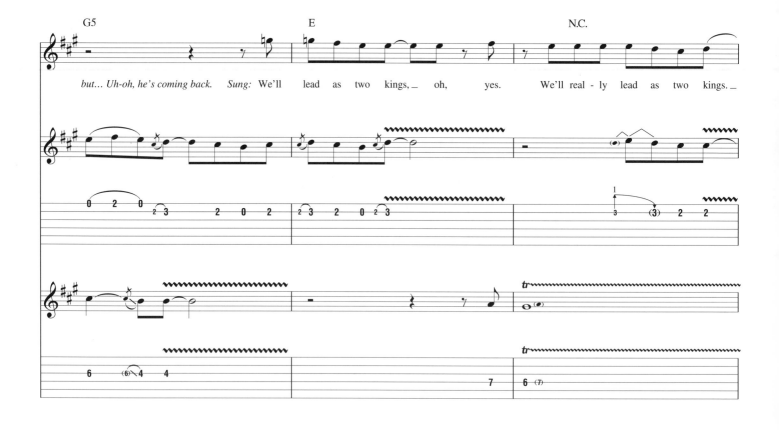

but... Uh-oh, he's coming back. *Sung:* We'll lead as two kings,_ oh, yes. We'll real-ly lead as two kings._

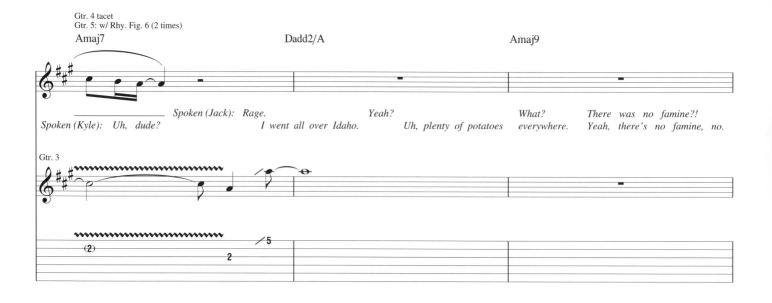

Gtr. 4 tacet
Gtr. 5: w/ Rhy. Fig. 6 (2 times)

Spoken (Jack): Rage.   Yeah?   What?   There was no famine?!
Spoken (Kyle): Uh, dude?   I went all over Idaho.   Uh, plenty of potatoes   everywhere.   Yeah, there's no famine, no.

Gtr. 3

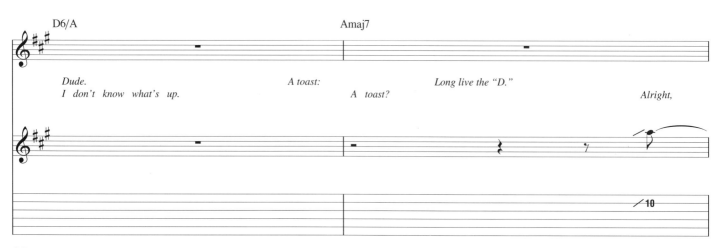

Dude.   A toast: Long live the "D."
I don't know what's up.   A toast?   Alright,

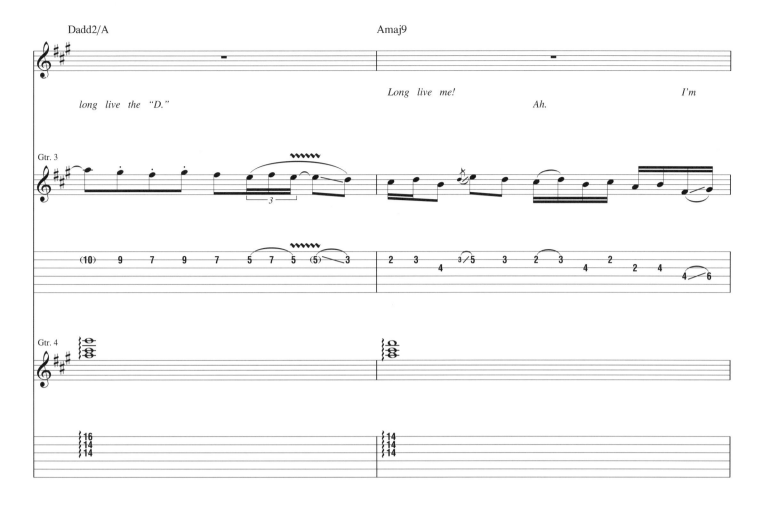

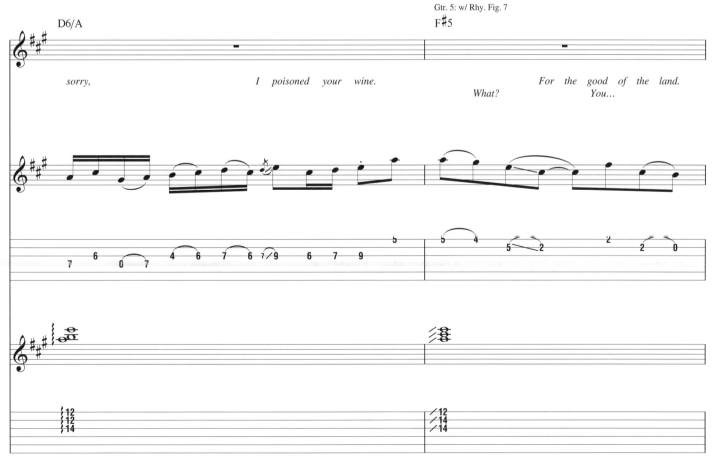

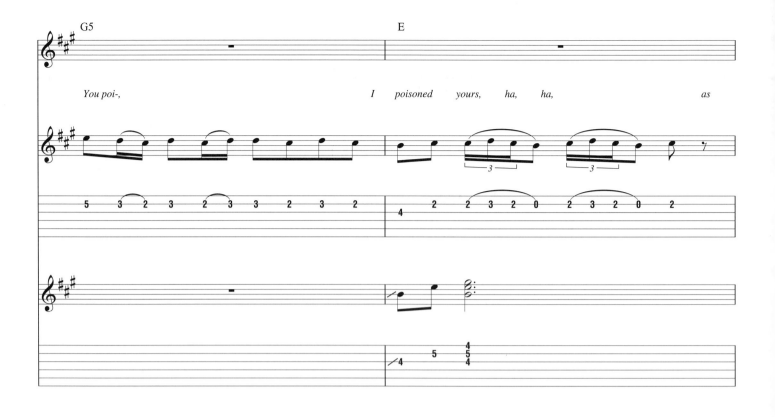

You poi-,   I   poisoned   yours,   ha,   ha,   as

Free time

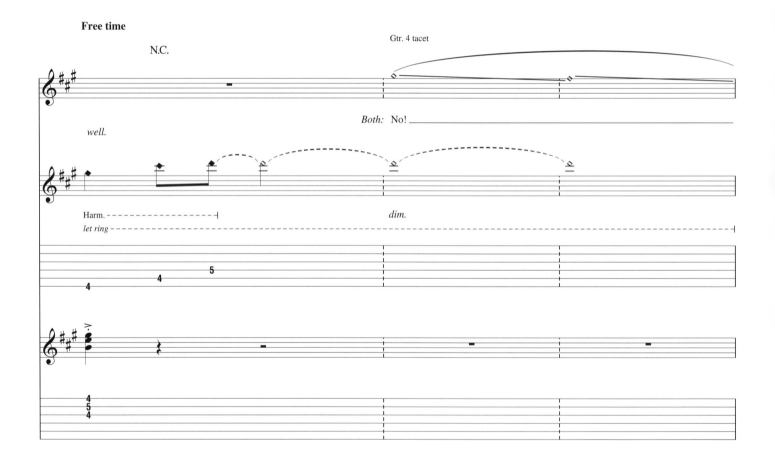

Gtr. 4 tacet

N.C.

well.

Both: No! ____

Harm.
let ring

dim.

Tempo II

Gtrs. 1 & 2: w/ Rhy. Fig. 1 (2 times)
Gtr. 3 tacet

Bkgd. Voc.: w/ shouting ad lib (next 6 meas.)
*Gtrs. 3 & 4: w/ Rhy. Fig. 1

A   F   G   A   F   G

___   *Jack:* No!

*w/ dist.

Bridge

Cit - y, cit - y, cit - y, cit - y, cit - y, cit - y, shit - ty. Shit - ty, cit - y, shit - ty,

shit - ty, cit - y, cit - y, shit - ty. Hall, hall, hall, hall, hall, hall, hall, hall!

Interlude
Tempo I

*Chord symbols reflect implied harmony.

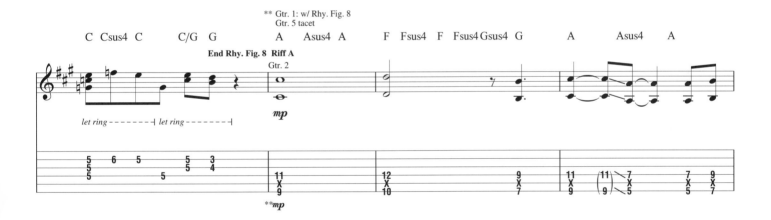

Outro

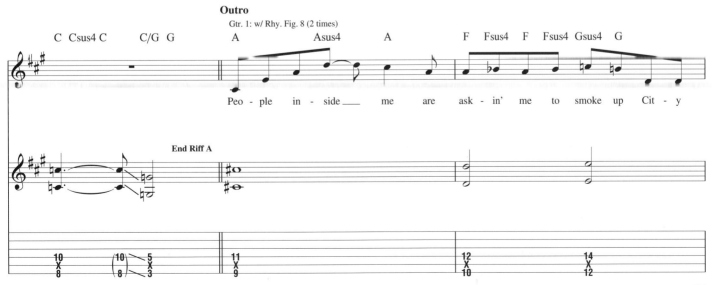

Peo - ple in - side ___ me are ask - in' me to smoke up Cit - y

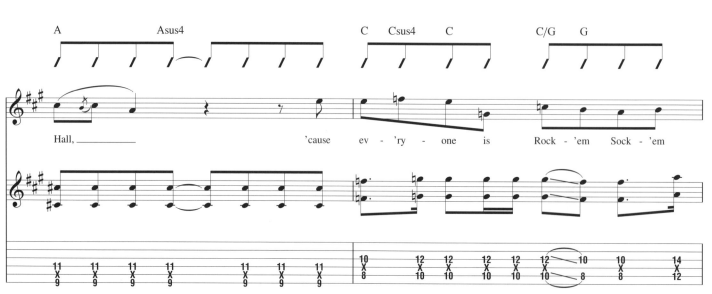

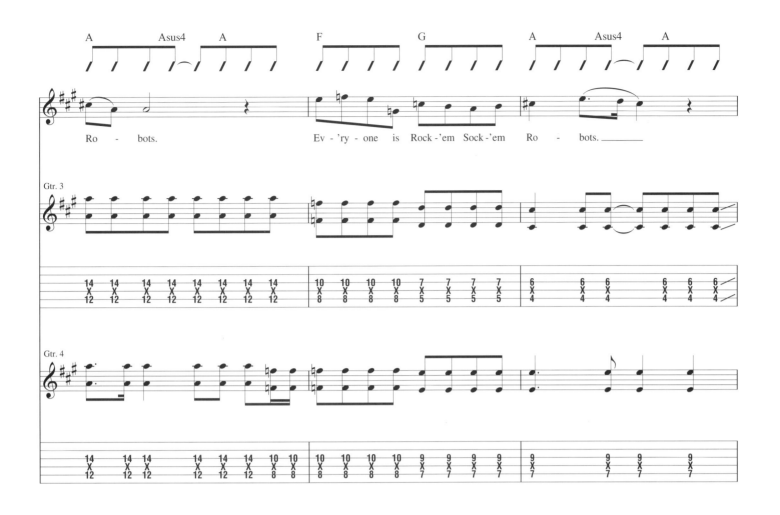

Ro - bots.   Ev - 'ry - one is Rock -'em Sock -'em   Ro - bots. ____

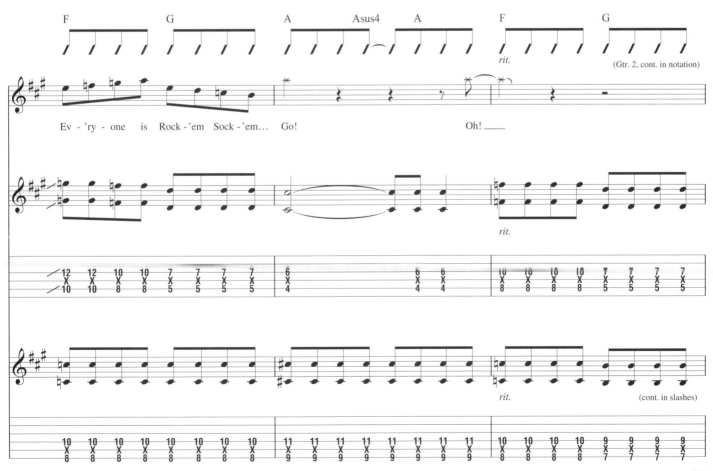

Ev - 'ry - one is Rock -'em Sock -'em...   Go!   Oh! ____

Free time

Jack: Don't... Cut that part out.

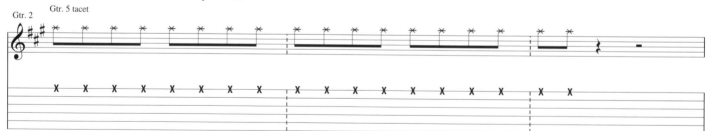

Moderately (♪♪ = ♪♪³)

Kyle: We've got it!

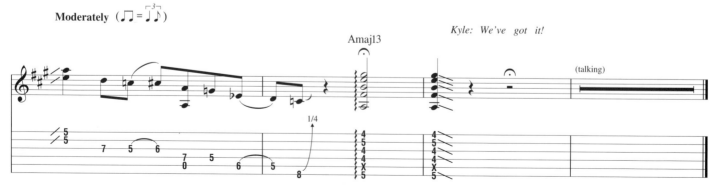

MALIBU NIGHTS

Words and Music by
Jack Black and Kyle Gass

Intro
Moderately fast ♩ = 172

*Kyle: Yeah, but you didn't fuckin'
come out with this one.*

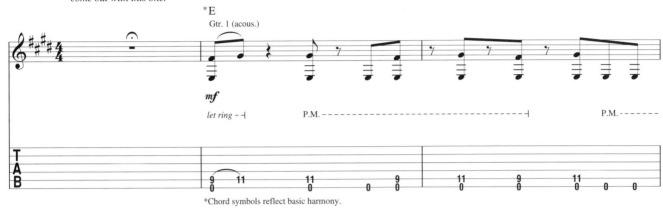

*Chord symbols reflect basic harmony.

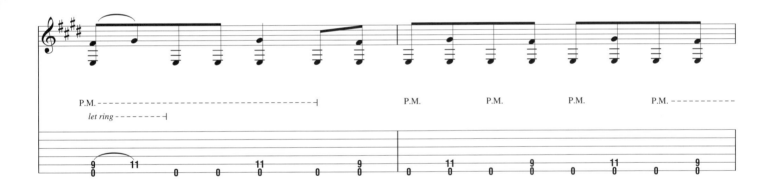

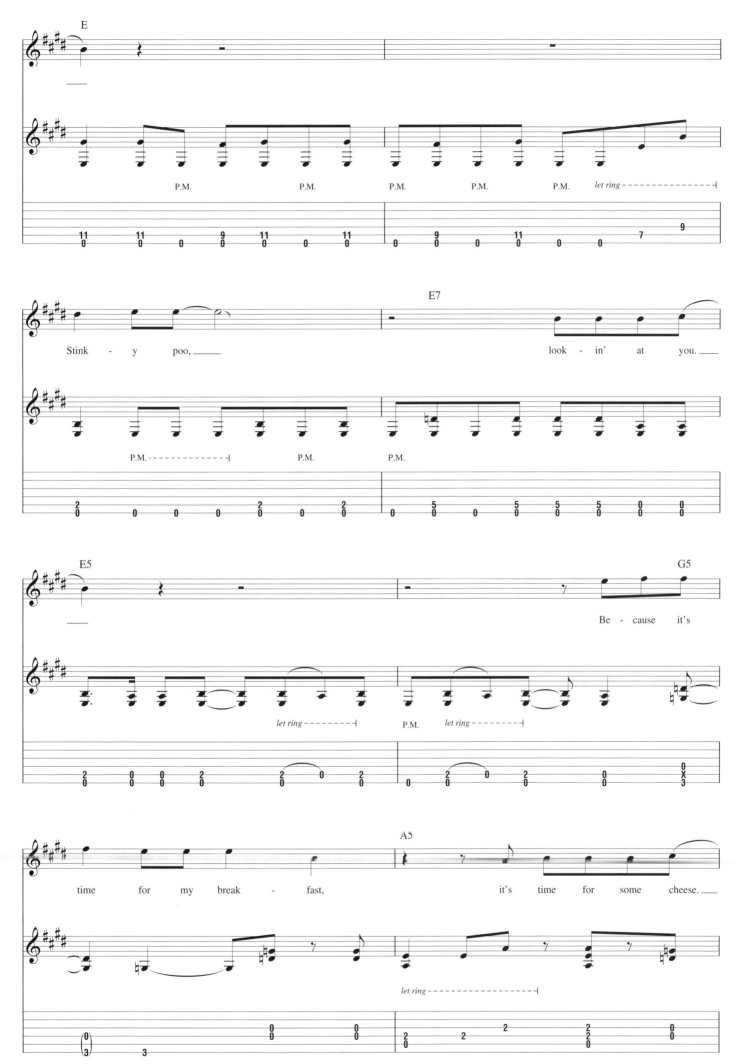